BOBBY ABEL

By the same author

KING LABOUR: THE BRITISH WORKING CLASS 1850–1914
THE SECRETARY OF STATE
THE CHANCELLOR OF THE EXCHEQUER

BOBBY ABEL

Professional Batsman

1857–1936

DAVID KYNASTON

"BOBBY"
AT
POINT

SECKER & WARBURG
LONDON

First published in England 1982 by
Martin Secker & Warburg Limited
54 Poland Street, London W1V 3DF

British Library Cataloguing in Publication Data
Kynaston, David
  Bobby Abel.
  1. Abel, Bobby   2. Cricket players—
  England—Biography
  I. Title
  796.35'8'0924   GV915.A/

ISBN 0-436-23951-5

Printed in Great Britain by
William Clowes Ltd, London and Beccles

*This book is dedicated to the memory of
Johnny Owen*

CONTENTS

LIST OF ILLUSTRATIONS

The line drawings appearing on the title page and in the text are from contemporary newspapers and are reproduced by kind permission of Surrey County Cricket Club and the British Library.

PREFACE

THE IDEA FOR this book came from hearing Jim Laker remark in a television commentary that Bobby Abel was known as 'the last of the specialist mid-ons'. It turns out that he usually fielded elsewhere, but I am grateful to the myth for getting me going. I have not attempted a full-scale, season-by-season biography of Abel, but rather an extended essay on his career as a professional cricketer. Ben Travers, who first saw Abel play in 1896, sent me shortly before he died in 1980 a charming letter, in which he described him as 'a top-level cricketer' and went on: 'No one could put him among the planets, but he permanently twinkles as a star. Anyhow, no littler cricketer can have been so great.'

Apart from the more familiar printed literature on the game, my main sources for this book have been threefold: the *Life and Reminiscences of Robert Abel in the Cricket Field*, which was published in 1910 and, apart from some pages on his early life, is little more than an unrevealing recapitulation of his batting achievements; the minutes of the Surrey club, which are deposited in the Surrey County Record Office at Kingston-upon-Thames; and the detailed match and tour reports contained in the contemporary press, most notably for my purposes in *The Times*, the *Sportsman*, the *Sporting Life*, the *Athletic News*, the *Star*, and *Cricket*, which papers account for the great majority of unattributed quotations in the text.

As far as a visual record of Abel is concerned, it is unfortunate that he had just ceased being a leading batsman at the time that Beldam undertook his major photographic examination of batting techniques and as a result is barely represented in his collection.

Some compensation lies in the existence of about half a minute of motion film of the Gentlemen and Players parading at Lord's in 1898, as shown to a suitably awestruck audience at the National Film Theatre in August 1981. Abel, however, is in camera for only a few seconds – and by the time that one starts to focus on him he has, like the horseman, passed by.

A lot of people have helped me one way and another. In addition to the Surrey club for allowing me to use their recently established library at the Oval, I would especially like to thank Ian Alister, Dianna Coward, Tim Curtis, Malcolm Falkus, Kate Gardiner, Tara Heinemann, Teresa McLean, Harry Ricketts, Nicholas Underhill, Andy Ward and Siân Whittaker.

'As the crowd waited for the game to stir into life in time it expanded into reminiscence. One man informed us – rather, he threw the news upon the morning air negligently – that he had witnessed Bobby Abel score 357 not out for Surrey against this very county of Somersetshire, in May 1889; he thought it was May but wouldn't swear to it. And another man informed us, but not negligently at all, that he had witnessed every run that Bobby Abel had ever scored in his life at Kennington Oval, so help him if he hadn't. This announcement was not, I think, widely accepted, but none the less the crowd was amenable; in its cosily huddled ranks fellow-feeling ran warm.'

Neville Cardus

'What suffering has he been through, and what happiness? Who is his God, and what in life or in death does he most fear? One wonders what he has worked at, and whether his wife is alive, and whether he has children. One wants desperately to pierce to the reality behind the clothes and talk, and it is only after one has been listening to him for some time that one begins to realize that the reality may lie precisely in those words "Abel", "boundary", "slow bowler", he is perpetually uttering.'

Dudley Carew (on an elderly spectator at the Oval)

'Even the usual founts of information, though, had no idea in April 1947 of what was to come. Indeed, one venerable man who had been on nodding terms with Bobby Abel gave it as his considered opinion – which he emphasized by switching from whisky to rum – that our visit to Worcester had coincided with the onset of the fifth Ice Age, and that it would probably be climatically impossible for cricket to be played in England for the ensuing ten thousand years.'

John Arlott

Chapter One

THE GUV'NOR

Who that ever saw it could forget that curious little figure, surmounted by a somewhat faded and shrunken chocolate cap, the slow half-waddling gait that marked its progress to the wicket, and then the mastery of technique that could reduce all but the very greatest bowlers to frustration?

Such is H. S. Altham's uncharacteristically lyrical description of a cricketer whose career figures command respect rather than awe. Between 1881 and 1904 Bobby Abel scored 32,669 runs for Surrey, England, and various representative teams in first-class matches at an average of 35.47. At the time of his retirement only Grace had made more runs. This aggregate included seventy-four centuries and a top score of 357 not out, a score which only MacLaren and Hutton amongst Englishmen have surpassed. Twice he established what were at the time records, in 1900 making twelve centuries and the following season scoring 3,309 runs. Abel was in fact a remarkably consistent batsman: if one takes the professional batting averages for the seventeen seasons from 1886 to 1902 inclusive, he was in the top three for thirteen of those seasons, including from 1894 to 1902 without a break. His test record was patchier. He played for England only thirteen times, all but twice against Australia, but did score 744 runs at an average of 37.20. Both his Test centuries were scored abroad: 120 at Cape Town in 1888–89, the first first-class century in South Africa, and 132 not out at Sydney in 1891–92, when he became the first of only three Englishmen to carry his bat against Australia. His overall figures, then, make him a batsman worth remembering, but alone they do not explain why he is remembered as fondly as he is.

'Abel was a tremendously popular personality, not only at the Oval: probably the most popular figure on the cricket field (except W. G. and Jessop) in the latter days of his career, at any rate in the South of England.' So Ben Travers recalled Abel in his heyday, round the turn of the century. From as early as 1884 he was known to the ring at the Oval as the 'Guv'nor', a friendly, semi-facetious term of endearment, which had come into general use as a mode of address to strangers from the 1850s and in Abel's case stuck to him as his nickname for the rest of his life. A typical instance of his general popularity occurred in 1893 when, following trouble with his eyes and a series of failures, he finally recovered his touch with a couple of good innings: at Old Trafford the Surrey batting 'was only redeemed by the satisfaction generally felt at the success of Abel', while versus Middlesex at Lord's a fortnight later 'it was quite like old times to see Abel playing all the bowling with ease and confidence' and he was 'deservedly applauded upon his retirement'. A notable tribute to his contemporary appeal was paid by *Vanity Fair* in 1902, when he became the first professional cricketer (following several amateurs) to be one of Spy's 'Men of the Day', with a full-page colour cartoon simply entitled 'Bobby'.

It was, however, specifically at the Oval that Abel had his most faithful, year-in year-out constituency. When he carried his bat for 136 versus Middlesex in 1894 'there was quite a personal feeling of satisfaction amongst the thousand present at the Oval at his triumph, for there is no more popular cricketer than Robert Abel'. Or, to quote from the closing words of that most sober of sources, the obituary columns of *Wisden* in 1937: 'After one of his great days at the Oval, hundreds of his admirers would gather in front of the pavilion and chant "Bob, Bob, Bob" again and again until the "Guv'nor" bowed his acknowledgements.'

C. B. Fry, writing in 1899 in *Giants of the Game*, put forward a typically acute explanation for this mass idolatry: 'He gathers runs like blackberries everywhere he goes, and is very popular on that account, and on the principle of "Go it, little 'un!" The average Cockney at the Oval suspects him of a wealth of cunning – "ikey" little dodges for outwitting the bowlers – and chuckles over all his strokes.' At five foot five inches Abel was indeed a little one and, by definition, likely to enlist a crowd's sympathies. In the words of the Sussex cricketer-turned-journalist W. A. Bettesworth, 'In a field in which nearly all the players are ever so much bigger than himself, he has the appearance of being a forlorn and innocent victim led forth to the slaughter.' And Bettesworth went on, 'So little fitted to take care of himself does he seem that when he is opposed to a fast bowler with a terrifying action, one half expects to see him carried away a mangled heap of humanity. Even when he has been at the wickets for hours, and the bowlers are completely worn out, he still looks innocent and unprotected – a humble little person who would be only too glad to retire into obscurity if he could get a chance.' Or, as Cardus in a late essay put it, 'He was, in fact, Strube's "Little Man", coping with international and home problems of cricket, long before Strube discovered him.'

Virtually all observers seem to have remarked on Abel's lack of inches, and the phrase 'the popular little Surrey professional' sounds like a keynote through the sporting journalism of the period. Foreign crowds were no exception, as at Melbourne in 1891: 'When Grace and Abel went out to open the innings of the Englishmen, the disparity of size was very remarkable. A funny man on the pavilion steps suggested Cain (the killer of bowlers) and Abel.' Not surprisingly, Abel himself felt a certain self-consciousness about his smallness. In his memoirs, in a rare moment of revelation about his first-class career, he noted of the giant Australian wicket-keeper J. McCarthy Blackham, 'On every possible occasion I avoided him in the field, the disparity in our heights and bulk always giving opportunity for the too evident, to me, amusement of the crowd.'

If he was somewhat sensitive about the constant harping on his slight physique, he may have been comforted by the words of the *Athletic News*, reviewing his record aggregate of 1901: 'Maybe Abel is not an Apollo and a Lionel Palairet rolled into one – but he is a mighty atom who has accomplished what neither Apollo or his near relative L. P. ever did.' Moreover, it is possible to exaggerate the physical deficiencies of the 9 st. 10 lbs atom. Fry again had some sensible words on the subject: 'As a matter of fact, there is nothing at all in Abel's build and constitution to prevent him from being a great batsman. He is not very tall, but, on the other hand, he has long arms and long legs for his size, and consequently is not deficient in reach.' It also seems that Abel had disproportionately large hands, which must presumably have been a considerable help. Moreover, five foot five inches was not in itself such a ridiculously small height for a professional cricketer of that time to be. Bagguley of Notts was reckoned at five foot three to be the shortest professional playing in the early 1890s, while Surrey's wicket-keeper during most of Abel's career, Harry Wood, was only five foot three and a half inches. And if, for instance, one takes the England team that played against Australia at Lord's in 1896, though of course

Abel was the smallest member, the average height was still only five foot nine inches. Yet whatever the precise relative statistics of the case, there remained something incorrigibly appealing about Abel as a physical presence on the cricket field. This was so even on his way out to bat, as an anthropologically minded Philadelphian spectator observed in 1901: 'Little Bobby Abel has a curious trick of pulling at the knee flaps of his pads as he leaves the pavilion and pulling his cap over his left eye.' While thirty years later R. L. Hodgson, the Country Vicar, recalled how he had 'liked his jaunty manner – his quaint, bird-like appearance (a mingling of the round-ness of a robin with the self-assertion of a cock-sparrow) – his sidelong waddle to and from the wicket'. And some time later E. H. D. Sewell of Essex, a former opponent, wrote of how 'Bobby Abel might almost be familiarly styled a dear little cricketer', and that 'there was something toy-like and droll about this little man as he waddled out to take guard'. In an era of tall, authoritative amateur batsmen, with an upright, military bearing, there was clearly some quality about the supremely unguardsmanlike Abel that touched a chord in his contemporaries.

As lovable toys go, though, this one met with remarkably few serious mishaps, a freedom from injury which Abel later attributed to the fact that from childhood he had been 'always very nimble and springy'. Probably his most significant actual injury was one, un-fortunately not stated what it was, that kept him out of the Test against Australia in 1888 at Sydney played by the two English touring teams combined. Only three times did he sustain serious hand injuries, much more seldom than one might have expected from a small opening batsman on often lively wickets: at Trent Bridge in 1886 he retired hurt (for the only time in his career) after getting 'a nasty blow on the thumb'; at Durban in 1889 he received a hand injury which turned into a sufficiently nasty sore to cause him to miss the following two matches versus Twenty-Two Cape Mounted Rifles; and in 1900 an injury to his left hand in net practice made him miss several of the early matches. Twice he received head injuries, but on neither occasion serious: in 1884 running into Wood (fielding out) in the deep in a Surrey versus Twenty-Four Colts match and being concussed; and two years later missing the rest of the day's play after stopping a return off his own bowling in a home match with Kent that for his pains gave him 'a fearful black eye'. Otherwise, the only significant injury inflicted to him on the cricket field occurred in 1896 when, again at Trent Bridge, a fast one from Guttridge struck him a bad blow on the chest and caused him to miss the next match.

As far as illness was concerned, Abel was again, apart from his eyes, similarly trouble-free. In 1884 an unstated illness caused him to miss several matches and then in 1900 an 'indisposition' made him miss another. A clue, perhaps, lies in the remark of the *Athletic News* correspondent reporting the home match with Gloucestershire in 1895, and in the process failing to avoid the most boring pun of the epoch: 'I was sorry to find Bob Abel disabled on Friday, with a bad attack of neuralgia, a complaint from which the little man often suffers.' Towards the end of his career he was also susceptible to chills, causing him in both 1900 and 1904 to miss one of the Hampshire matches. In general, however, he maintained his physical stamina remarkably well throughout his career: it is true that in 1897, after batting almost the whole day with Brockwell to set up a new first-wicket record of 379, he was out next ball failing 'to recover his ground after going out to play Wynyard's slows . . . thoroughly done up as he owned to be', thereby falling short of the then record for all wickets; but two years later, at the age of forty-one, he 'did not appear in the least fatigued' in the course of making his monumental triple century against Somerset. If his speed and reflexes in the field perhaps began to decline in the course of the 1890s, his physical as well as mental capacity for making large scores certainly did not.

What really caused Abel his physical problems were his eyes, most dramatically in the spring of 1893 when they succumbed to a rheumatic infection in the wake of diphtheria. He recalled:

For five days I was blind. Then Mr Boyington, the county scorer, saw me, and at once went to the county authorities, who wired to Dr Critchett, the famous oculist, asking if he would see me on the next day – a Sunday. This was an unusual thing for him to do, but he kindly consented. He made me sit for an hour with something in my eye, to see whether it acted on the pupil. At the end of this time he said, 'It is all right, and I can make you see again, but if you had come to me only a day later you would have been permanently blind in the left eye.' In about a week I could open my eyes and could see, and in about three weeks my sight was strong again.

Abel's subsequent re-entry into the first-class orbit was not easy,
missing the first three matches of the season and then making only
six runs in five innings, culminating in a pair against the Australians,
being run out in the second innings following a bad call from W. H.
Lockwood. He then missed the next two matches, but, after taking
a century off Guy's Hospital for the Club and Ground, made his 54
not out at Old Trafford and 45 at Lord's. His form for the rest of
the season was uneven, but the great mid-career crisis had been
surmounted, in a way somewhat analogous to Hobbs' appendicitis
in 1921. The palmiest nine seasons of Abel's cricketing life lay
immediately ahead and during them he amassed over 20,000 runs.
Eye trouble returned decisively in 1903, but by then he would
probably not have had much more time left as a top-class batsman
anyway.

There was more, however, to Abel's popularity than merely an
appreciation of how he had overcome the handicaps of his smallness
and his rheumy eyes. His whole background was a subject ripe for a
generation which still relished real life self-help stories portrayed in
the classic Samuel Smiles mould. 'Few young professionals have,
perhaps, in so short a time, won a deservedly high position under
such difficulties and with apparently such slight promise at the
outset of their careers,' wrote *Cricket* in 1885, stressing that Abel
had 'learnt his cricket under far from favourable conditions'. Five
years later *Wisden* expanded the theme, declaring that 'his present
high position among professional cricketers may be described as
a triumph of perseverance'. By the turn of the century this song
of praise was being repeated with almost monotonous regularity,
culminating in the pen portrait in *Vanity Fair* accompanying
Spy's cartoon: 'He improves with age; for he is quite a self-made
player . . . But he believes in himself, and pluck and perseverance
have brought him to his present high estate.' And if one considers
that not only was he a shining example of a cricketing autodidact,
but also that he was, as far the Surrey crowd was concerned, a local
boy made good, then it is clear that even without his appealing
physical appearance he would almost certainly have been, in the
phrase of the day, the 'pet' of the Ovalites.

Robert Abel was born on 30 November 1857 at 18 Commercial
Street in Rotherhithe. His father was Thomas Abel, a lamp-lighter;

and his mother, Elizabeth, signed the birth certificate with a mark over four weeks after the event. Rotherhithe was very much part of nineteenth-century dockland and Commercial Street itself lay just to the south of Albion Pond, Canada Pond, and Quebec Pond. As an area to grow up in it was not the safest place in the world, in that it was estimated in 1865 that almost half the deaths in Rotherhithe that year were of children under five; but later in the century Charles Booth wrote of the district that 'in spite of bad sanitation health is wonderfully good, for the people live largely in the open air, and the air at Rotherhithe, between river, park and docks, is wholesome and good to breathe.' Two of Abel's main youthful interests were pigeon-fancying and, later on, step-dancing, at which he won a four-guinea silver cup in a competition held at the local St Helena Gardens. 'As usual, my nerves troubled me at first, but when I got going I felt like going on for weeks.' But virtually right from the start cricket does seem to have been his great passion, playing it in the streets and using the lights as wickets.

His first big break occurred in 1869 with the opening of Southwark Park, laid out on the old market gardens of Rotherhithe and situated only a stone's throw away from Commercial Street. It comprised sixty-three acres in all, part of it was specifically a cricket ground, and from a young cricketer's point of view it must have been like the proverbial manna. It was to the park that he and his friends 'repaired on every possible occasion. Three days a week matches were played on the centre of the ground. This drove our Bohemian brotherhood to the sides, but on the other three days we were allowed to pitch anywhere.' Not that the park was flawless. Thirteen years after it had opened the *South London Press* noted that, 'The cricket ground, especially on a Saturday afternoon, is really dangerous to enter, so small is the space allotted for the pastime,' and that, 'This is the less excusable that there are large portions of the ground left in a condition in which they are available neither for cricket nor for any other purpose.' While as to the sort of terrain on which he learnt his cricket, Abel recalled that, 'The match portion was rough enough, but the sides of the ground were such that a ball might either break a yard or rear up clean over the batsman's head.' And, inevitably: 'Batting one day on the rough ground, a ball rose and hit me full in the face. Breaking my nose, and fracturing my jaw, it twisted my nose round to my right cheek.

My nose did not look like a nose at all.' But after he had had his nose straightened out and plastered in position, within a few days he was back playing in the park, 'bandages and all' – not thanks to Thomas Abel, who 'never cottoned to cricket' and after the accident told his son that he would thrash him if he ever caught him at the game again. Encouragement instead came from the Surrey opener Tom Humphrey:

> He happened to be in the park one day when I was practising with other small boys. After a time he said: 'Here, let me give you a ball, youngster!' and then asked me to bowl to him for a few minutes. I can only remember one thing he said to me, but I have never forgotten this. He told me that when I wanted to hit I ought to get well to the pitch of the ball. I believe that that remark has had a great deal to do with the way in which I have generally managed to keep the ball down.

Abel's first proper match was probably played on Peckham Rye at the age of about fifteen. 'A Mr Peters of Mr Bevington's [the well-known firm in the leather trade at Bermondsey] had noticed me while playing at Southwark Park. One day they asked me to play for Bevington's Cricket Club. I did, and was bowled first ball. They asked me to play again, but I was so utterly disgusted with myself that I shunned these gentlemen as if they were my enemies.' But Peters continued to believe in Abel's potential and, at the most within a year or two of the Peckham Rye débâcle, got him elected a member of the Southwark Park Cricket Club and even paid his subscription:

> All the players were men, and I felt very much out of it at first. My first match for the club was against Kingston, who had a strong batting team. I fielded out the whole of the day from eleven o'clock to seven. A bat was offered every season for the highest batting average among the members of the Southwark Park Club. For eleven years in succession this had been won by Mr John White, a publican, of Spa Road, Bermondsey. He used to exhibit these prize bats in his bar. In my first season I won this bat by beating the proud possessor of the eleven bats by a decimal, to his great annoyance.

Unfortunately the local press failed to print the club's scores, but apparently during these formative six or seven seasons Abel did not score a century, at least on his home ground. The *Sporting Life* in 1880 refers to a Wednesday afternoon match played 'on a wretched wicket' in Southwark Park against Richmond and, though giving no individual scores, mentions that Abel's fielding 'deserves a word of praise'. And though White again won the prize bat for the 1880 season, Abel's performances that year must have been reasonably impressive, since at some point then three of Surrey's professionals, Barratt, Johnson, and Boardman, apparently advised him 'to go up for the Colts' and try to secure a place on the Oval ground staff. But for the moment Abel preferred to bide his time.

Almost certainly he did so because of the influence exercised on him by a Mr Wrigley, a Yorkshireman who was an even more important patron of the young Abel than Peters of Bevington's. The exact chronology is again uncertain, but Wrigley entered Abel's life after the match at Peckham Rye and probably before he joined Southwark Park CC:

> One day, while I was practising on Southwark Park, the Boro' Hop Trade Cricket Club were playing Willow Walk, and were a man short. I was asked to make up the side, which I did after a lot of persuasion. To say that I was in a blue funk when I went in to bat for the Hop Club after a collapse is the simplest manner in which I can describe my feelings. However, I went in, and with a Mr Wrigley helped to pull the game out of the fire. My 24 was top score, Mr Wrigley making 20. Mr Wrigley, who held the position of foreman in a large hop warehouse [Bakers, White & Morgan], at once offered me a situation, so that I could play with him and his principal's sons. They were really good sportsmen and I not only played cricket all the summer for the club belonging to the firm, but in the winter in one of the warehouses.

In other words, from the ages of about sixteen to twenty-two Abel was playing on a regular basis for the Bakers, White & Morgan team as well as for Southwark Park itself. Nor was this all, for at some point during these years – in 1880 according to one version of the story, rather earlier according to another – Abel made what was probably his debut at the Oval:

A Mr Freeland – an hotel proprietor in South London – was very anxious that the South of the Thames Licensed Victuallers should beat the North of the Thames Licensed Victuallers in the annual match at the Oval. Mr Freeland approached me to play as his son. I played a good innings, and was told that Mr Alcock [the Secretary] was so pleased with my display that he asked, 'Who is that youngster?' 'Young Freeland,' was the reply. 'No; that's not young Freeland; it's young Abel from Southwark Park.' During the luncheon I was seated opposite Mr Freeland, and kept addressing him as 'father'. Mr Alcock subsequently came to Southwark Park, and asked me if I would like to go up for the Colts, but I told him that Mr Wrigley did not think I was a good enough player, and that when I was he would recommend me.

Finally, in the early months of 1881, Abel came to the conclusion that enough was enough of Yorkshire caution (or perhaps possessiveness) and decided to go for broke. In January that year he married Sarah Reffell, the daughter of a rope-maker, at the Parish Church in St Martin-in-the-Fields. His address on the marriage certificate was given as 7 Mercer Street, hers as 22 Mercer Street: it was presumably a Seven Dials romance. And three months later, under threat from Wrigley of losing his job, but with a recommendation from the Southwark Park Club, he did go up for the Colts at the Oval. No doubt it was at this stage that his date of birth became 30 November 1859, a date perpetuated in the reference books until the 1920s: to have gone up for the Colts at the age of twenty-three would have been at best ridiculous, at worst impermissible.

Throughout his subsequent career Abel maintained close links with the area where he had grown up and then moved back to when he got married, living in Raymouth Road up to about 1884 and then Pedworth Road. His following in Rotherhithe and Bermondsey was always strong. For instance, shortly before he sailed to the Cape in 1888, friends gave him a farewell evening at the Prince Alfred in Bermondsey, at which 'the chair was filled by Mr W. Brown, who

made a very telling speech, which was feelingly responded to by
"Bobby", and received with uproarious applause'; while on his
return five months later he received from his local admirers a
handsome clock-barometer in recognition of his achievements. Soon
afterwards he settled near to the Oval, first in Trigon Road and then
some time later in Handforth Road, but each year from 1891 to 1904
he brought his own team (usually including one or two other Surrey
professionals) to Southwark Park at the end of the season to play
a match against local cricketers. Invariably several thousands
attended and a collection was made for charitable purposes, up to
1899 for the aged Charlie Farr, who for many years had been
groundsman at Southwark Park and had given Abel some of his
earliest informal tuition. 'Vociferous cheering' usually greeted Abel
going out to bat on these occasions and twice he obliged with
centuries. In 1891, though, 'the ground being anything but good, he
went in for a lively game, and caused much amusement by a lot of
very short runs, but the laugh went somewhat against him when he
got a man neatly run out'. Usually the participants and some of the
spectators adjourned afterwards to a nearby pub for speeches and a
smoking concert. Typical was the evening of the 1893 match. Abel
sat to the right of the chairman, who, after expressing gratitude for
the services he had given to Farr's benefit, introduced him:

> Cheer after cheer was given, and it was some minutes before
> Mr Abel could get a chance to speak. Eventually he said it
> gave him very great pleasure to come amongst his old friends
> once again . . . He would never be backward in coming to
> Southwark Park on such an occasion, but he hoped that the
> next time he came the cricket pitches might be planed down a
> little . . . He thanked the company for the grand reception
> they had given him and his brother professionals, and resumed
> his seat amidst hearty cheers.

Then came the songs, during which 'Charlie Chambers was
extremely good in his original encore song, "Fancy That", in which
he introduced some very humorous verses, one respecting Abel and
his dog going remarkably well'. The dog in question may well have
been Abel's own, but quite possibly it referred to an episode that
had been reported a few days earlier in a match at Reigate between

Grace's Eleven and W. W. Read's Eleven. 'Not the least amusing incident of the afternoon was the appearance of a little dog on the field. This little animal followed Abel from slip to long-off and back at the end of each over for the best part of an hour, and could not be induced to leave the Surrey professional.'

Perhaps dogs are good judges of character, for there is no evidence that Abel ever made any enemies on or off the field. 'A kindly man' was how Andrew Sandham years later recalled the Abel of the 1900s, while the wicket-keeper A. A. Lilley remembered how amidst the schoolboys at the Oval his autograph 'was given with as much pleasure as it was received by the boys, some of whom were quite as big as the great little Bobby himself'. John Shuter, who captained Surrey during the first half of Abel's career and also opened with him, wrote in his introduction to Abel's reminiscences that 'Nothing ruffled his invariable good temper, and in all the years that I was associated with him I cannot recall one single instance in which he showed the slightest sign of discontent or grumbling.' Or, as *Wisden* put it in his obituary: 'Quiet and unassuming in manner, Abel was never spoiled by success.' Yet there was rather more to his character than simply kindliness and phlegmatic modesty. Someone who clearly relished his whole *persona* was Fry, whose 1899 description of Abel included this brief but suggestive passage:

> His face is ruddy and wrinkled, and suggests premature age or many cares. He has the peculiar serious expression common to grooms and music-hall artists; one is never quite certain whether he has just lost a dear relative or is on the point of saying something very funny. He never smiles even after he has passed his second century. But he has the reputation of being a jester of the first water.

One form this jesting could take was in the singing of comic songs, as in the latter stages of the dinner given in Colombo in 1891 to the touring party on its way to Australia. 'Briggs, Read, and Abel sang, Abel being very funny, and fairly brought down the house.' Not that Abel's singing was universally appreciated, for later on the same tour the *Sporting Life*'s correspondent expressed the opinion that the constant round of receptions, with their 'everlasting praise, and gush, and drink, and soft tack', was actually 'worse than sitting

in a smoking carriage, grouped round Bobby Abel, with him leading the rest in part songs'. What evidence there is rather suggests
that his sense of humour was of the quizzical, fatalistic variety, the
humour almost of passivity. H. D. G. Leveson-Gower told the story
of how one year, probably near the very end of Abel's career, his
own eleven was playing a match at Limpsfield against a local team
that included the fledgling Neville Knox. Opening with Abel was
W. G., who for once broke with his usual custom. ' "You take first
ball this time, Bobby," Grace said, "so that I can have a look at this
young fast bowler." "Thank you kindly, sir," Bobby said wryly,
and obeyed.'

Abel's roots were deeply urban and the various accounts of him on
tour depict him as the very antithesis of the intrepid pioneer type.
The voyage out to Australia in 1887 was probably his first time at
sea, which no doubt accounts for the deck-scene at Plymouth just
before departure including Abel 'meeting with a "running fire" of
chaff from his fellow-professionals'. He was, in fact, a reasonable
sailor, though on the first full day of the trip out to Australia in 1891,
going through the Bay of Biscay, he did not make an appearance
until dinner in the evening, 'being a little queer', though 'not very
bad'. On that second Australian tour (much better documented
than the earlier one) Abel nearly met an unfortunate end, when at
Gippsland, hardly having ridden on horseback before, he decided
to join in some kangaroo-hunting. 'Bobby cut an amusing figure
mounted on a fleet little pony, to which he had to cling with one
hand in front and the other behind the saddle.' In fact the pony
bolted at the first sight of a kangaroo, crashed under some trees, and
was only just pulled up by Abel before a hidden wire fence would
have had him thrown off.

During the tour he seems to have been recognized as the choicest
victim of all the practical joking that was going, starting as early as
the voyage out. He and Sharpe shared the same cabin. As Alfred
Shaw recalled:

It was a known weakness of Abel's that he had no liking for
rats. With the aid of Attewell, Peel manoeuvred a piece of
string across Abel's bunk while he was attempting to get some
rest. The manipulation of this in the darkness suggested to

Abel the pranks of the detested rodents, and it was rare fun to
Peel and Attewell to hear him jump up in his berth, shout
'Jack, Jack, there they are again,' and proceed to strike round
the bunk at the imagined objects of his terror and disgust.

In Australia the gambit of putting a dead snake in Abel's cricket
bag had a similar desired effect, while on the way back, according to
Grace's narrative, the main joke on Abel was played in Aden:

While waiting for mails we amused ourselves by fishing and
caught a number of fish with prickly fins and a sort of spike
near their gills. My son caught several of the fish, which I took
off the hooks. In doing so the fish stabbed my hand with their
spikes. While we were fishing, Abel came on deck, and one of
the members of our team picked up a fish and dropped it over
Bobby's shoulder. Somehow the fish got its spike into his leg,
and stuck there. Bobby, who had been told that the fish
belonged to a poisonous variety, was in an awful funk. Bean
sucked the wound, and, as Bobby thought, saved his life.
Then he was put to bed, and poultices were ordered, but poor
Bobby was inconsolable, until I showed him the wound which
the fish had made in my hand, and assured him the fish were
harmless, as, of course, they were.

Much more physically rigorous, though, than either Australian
tour was the Cape enterprise of 1888–89. Major Warton's team was
the first touring side to go to South Africa, so, unlike the Australian
tours that Abel went on, there was no tried and tested procedure
already in existence. Obviously unaware of what lay ahead, Abel
was in fact 'in extremely good spirits and positively skittish' as the
team prepared to sail from Blackwall. And in the course of the tour
he did willingly engage in a couple of outdoor adventures, though
neither time with conspicuous success. Once, under the auspices of
a local landowner, he went buck-shooting with Johnny Briggs and
Maurice Read, as Read recalled:

Mr Deane posted us in various positions, sending twenty or
thirty Zulus to beat up the buck. Abel and Briggs were placed
together. Briggs got off his horse and loaded his rifle, but Abel

forgot to unstrap his and kept on his horse. Suddenly a buck jumped up right in front of them, and Briggs let off his weapon. The shots went over a tree. In the meantime Abel was frantically tugging to unfasten his musket, and succeeded in doing so when the buck was miles and miles away.

His other adventure was also with Briggs. The two of them enjoyed catapult-shooting, 'breaking street lamps and "potting" at the natives', and one day, finding themselves near a large plantation of young trees, went in and with their knives started making catapult sticks from the trees. Whereupon 'a brawny nigger well over six feet high came along with a gun', they started to run, and Briggs, who outpaced Abel, was just about to jump over the fence when he heard a cry of ' "Don't leave me to be scalped alone!" ' They were then taken to an officer, but on their identities being revealed everything turned out fine.

What really dominated the tour, however, was the travel, in which seemingly no mode of transport was left unused. 'There were a dozen horses to rattle us along, and off we started across the veldt at a pace that brought a rigid expression on to Bobby Abel's features. How that coach jolted, jumped, and swayed!' Such was the start of the 300 miles 'of rough coach travelling' that took the party from Kimberley to Johannesburg. Three weeks later and the team was on its way by train from Pietermaritzburg to Durban. 'The sea coast and the scenery on the way was simply beautiful; the railroad running in and out among the hills – at an incline generally of 1 in 30 – and swerving round deep dongas in an alarming manner at times, caused poor little "Bobby" to sit tight.' While after the match at Durban the team went on by ship:

Arriving alongside the *Drummond Castle* the usual rope ladder and basket scene took place . . . Abel, whose legs so firm on the cricket ground are always shaky on the sea, took hold of the ropes about a dozen times, but the ladder was too much for him, and 'Bobby' was finally induced to be hoisted in the basket as the safest mode of being put on board.

However, prior to these illustrious episodes the real epic of the tour had already taken place, namely the journey from Port

Elizabeth to Oudtshoorn. The first stage, by sea, was no problem,
but then came the part that sorted out the men from the mice. In the
words again of one of the accompanying journalists, this time from
the *Sportsman*:

> Reaching Mossel Bay somewhat later than we had expected,
> and being anxious to press on to George Town that night, we
> seated ourselves at once in the six Cape carts which were to take
> us as far as Oudtshoorn. Shortly after striking inland we found it
> becoming very dark and rain came on heavily. Our 'Cape carts'
> were not provided with lamps, so that our pace here and there
> was much reduced. After an hour's journeying we were over-
> taken by Mr Barry, of Oudtshoorn, with a cart provided with
> lamps. He at once showed the way and we got along much
> better till a shout from the rear stopped us. The last cart, with
> Bobby Abel and Fothergill, could not be seen anywhere. So we
> go back on foot. At last a plaintive cry is heard through the
> darkness, and we find they have narrowly escaped an upset,
> and have gone off the road. Poor little Abel is in a terrible state
> of fear, declaring 'them precipices' to be too much for any man's
> peace of mind. All right once more, and reach Brak River at
> 10.20, where we outspan, and hearing that the road beyond is
> very dangerous, we decide to stay there till daybreak.

Abel's reminiscences reveal precisely why the party decided to
stay that night at the Temperance Hotel on the Brak River:

> Major Warton wanted to continue the journey a few miles
> further, which meant climbing a mountain 5,000 feet high. I
> got him into a quiet corner and implored him to stay where we
> were for the night. 'It's as well to be killed at once as frightened
> to death,' I said. He was at first immovable, but on my telling
> him I would not go any further that night even if he sent me
> back to England he relented. When we scaled the mountain
> at daybreak, we found we had to travel round the edge of a
> precipice – a sheer drop of 350 feet.

Nor, despite the daylight, was the next day a doddle, though by
the end of it the tourists finally got to Oudtshoorn. On the way, after

going through George Town, they reached a Dutch shanty called the North Station Hotel and there obtained some food. But: ' "Where is the sixth cart with Abel and Fothergill?" "Many a mile behind" it appeared, and half an hour later they arrived wet to the skin. They had done the last two miles on foot, their horses having broken down, and to make the best of things had been blackberrying on the way.' Gathering blackberries like runs was, no doubt, thin consolation for not being safely ensconced in the great indoors of 14 Pedworth Road, SE.

Yet it is perhaps too easy to mock, for there was another aspect to this keenly developed instinct for self-preservation. As Abel told Bettesworth in 1897:

> To become a cricketer, more especially nowadays, you have to do something to keep your place. I have been one of the comparatively few fortunate ones able to keep their place for years, but to do this I have had to give up everything else. I sacrifice everything for cricket, never stop out late, and always take the greatest care of myself.

Examples are legion of professionals of the period who failed to take care of themselves, but simply to quote from *Wisden*'s obituary of Peate, who stopped playing for Yorkshire in 1887 at the age of thirty-one: 'Without using a harsh word, it may fairly be said that he would have lasted longer if he had ordered his life more carefully.' Indeed, it is noteworthy that if one looks at the rest of the Players team of 1886 with whom Abel played his first match against the Gentlemen at Lord's, the nearest in longevity to Abel's seventy-nine was Maurice Read, who attained the age of seventy. Moreover, closely related to physical dedication was his mental attitude. Again in Abel's own words, looking back in 1902 on his career: 'Whenever I got out, I set myself to study the how and why until I discovered how I should have played the ball that beat me. This practice I still follow.' While Strudwick once recollected how he had 'seen Bobby Abel come in after making 200, go straight in front of the mirror, and play the shot again that got him out'. And Strudwick also remembered how on another occasion he himself had gone out to bat with over 400 on the board and had been reproached for getting out to a careless stroke: ' "The bowlers are tired, Struddy," Abel

said, "you could have stayed and got a lot of runs." ' He was
certainly not one of the game's walkers, as the correspondent of the
Athletic News noted in 1889:

> I have seldom seen a worse decision than that in the Surrey *v*
> Middlesex match when the umpire gave Abel not out for a
> catch at the wicket. As far away as the press-room we could
> hear the 'click' clearly, and Abel himself afterwards openly
> admitted that he hit the ball hard.

Three years later, in a festival match at Hastings, 'Abel did not at
all like the decision' when he was run out for 117. Making runs was
his living: his attitude to it was as simple as that. As Ranji/Fry put it
in their *Jubilee Book*, for all his being 'a curious little fellow with a
slow, jerky gait and a serio-comic cast of countenance', nevertheless
'he is all there – a tough nut to crack'. Or, as C. M. Wells once
remarked to Pelham Warner while in the field for Middlesex against
Surrey: 'How awful! The "Guv'nor" has sent for his sun hat; that
means he will be here all day.'

Chapter Two

SURREY'S PRIDE

Abel makes one of a long line of distinguished Surrey batsmen.
Maurice Read and he, when Surrey's prospects were darkest and no
new batsmen from the professional ranks seemed likely to take up the
mantle of Jupp and Pooley, came to the rescue and revived the race of
professional batsmen in the South of England, which at that time
appeared to be dying out.

THE HON. R. H. LYTTELTON, not one of the Guv'nor's greatest
admirers, here gives an accurate perspective to the context in which
Abel emerged during the 1880s as a major batsman. Surrey were
indeed in the doldrums: having been in the 1850s and early 1860s
probably the most powerful county, during the 1870s they only in
one season won more matches than they lost; and in 1880, the year
of Maurice Read's debut and on the eve of Abel's, they won only
two matches against other counties, drew five, and lost seven. As
Lyttelton implied, Surrey's decline was intimately bound up with
their lack of professional batsmen. Whereas in 1852 nine of the
Surrey team that defeated England were professionals, and during
the great period that followed there were usually about eight
professionals in the side, by the early 1870s there seems to have
occurred a decisive change of policy. Some years afterwards the
prominent cricket writer Frederick Gale ('The Old Buffer') recalled
how in 1873 he had resigned from Surrey's match committee 'in
utter disgust at the apathy of the amateurs towards young professionals, and worse than apathy, their running them down, and
putting themselves and their friends in all matches when there was
easy bowling, and at their great disinclination to go out and appear
before a Yorkshire or Nottingham ring'. 'In fact,' wrote Gale, 'I
have no hesitation in saying that the reign of the amateurs ruined
the county.'

By the beginning of the 1880s, however, it was realized that the
county needed in the long term a stronger leavening of professional
talent, a realization that resulted in the last week of April 1881 in a
pioneering scheme. One of Grace's books, *Cricket*, described it well:

19

The committee invited colts from all parts of the county to practise at the Oval under the eyes of good and competent judges. The old arrangement of having a colts' match once or twice a year had not produced favourable results, many a promising colt failing to do himself justice through nervousness or some other cause. Constant practice for a week was a better test and showed whether they had the making of county players in them.

There were two key figures behind this scheme. One was Frederick Burbidge, who had played for Surrey from 1854 to 1866, thereafter served on the committee, and was now the principal initiator of the week's trials. To assist him Burbidge secured the help of the Hon. Robert Grimston, who was now in his sixties, but who, after playing for Harrow and Oxford, had in the 1840s been one of the founders of I. Zingari as well as of the Surrey club itself. In Gale's words, 'Mr Grimston had for many years become estranged from the club, but, for the sake of cricket, came to the rescue, and in unusually cold and bleak April weather he came day by day and reviewed the young candidates for fame, saw them practise together, formed sides, umpired for them, and coached them, as he did the Harrow boys.' Sixty young cricketers attended the week of 'test practice' and for doing so received 'reasonable expenses' from the Surrey executive.

Abel recalled: 'I went up for the Colts. Just as any one who has learnt to cycle on a crock realizes the difference when he mounts a high grade machine, so did I realize the difference between a park cricket ground and the true level turf of the Oval.' Precise details are not known, but Abel did well enough under Grimston's supervision to play in the middle of May, first for Surrey's Young Professionals against her Young Amateurs at the Oval and then for Surrey Colts versus Kent Colts at Maidstone. Though played in these matches primarily as a batsman, he shone in both of them much more as a bowler, taking 10 for 54 and 16 for 51 respectively. 'Surrey unearths a new slow bowler' was apparently one of the press headlines; and on the strength of his performances he was engaged as a ground bowler. Over the next few weeks Abel continued to play for Southwark Park as well as Surrey Colts and Surrey Club and Ground, taking, for instance, seven wickets against Limehouse for his old team on 18 June. In general his performances under his new auspices were not startling, though at the end of May he did make 75 in a Club and Ground match against Putney. *Cricket* later recalled those early days at the Oval: 'When he first came under the notice of the Surrey authorities his cricket was very crude. None the less the smartness he showed in the field, and his evident anxiety to improve his play, afforded hopes that he would develop into a good, all-round cricketer.'

On 21 July, versus Nottinghamshire at the Oval, Abel made his his county debut. He was drafted in at the last moment, various amateurs being unable to play, and apparently his 'introduction into the Surrey eleven was regarded by many practical players and capable critics as anything but a display of good judgement'. Surrey batted first and at about half past four Abel went in with the score 273 for 7. 'I do not know how I got to the crease. My bat felt like a shovel and as heavy as lead.' He made a single, but was then, in the words of *The Times*, 'overcome by a ball from Mills' and bowled. That was his only innings, as Surrey crushed an under-strength Notts side by an innings, but he did get two wickets and caught Gunn off a skier. He played twice more for Surrey during the season, both times against Sussex. At the Oval he made 1 and 3, at Hove 0 and 12. Batting at number six in that final innings, and lasting while four wickets fell at the other end, Abel's top first-class score to date was not a comfortable affair: though making a couple of on-side fours, he 'survived an appeal for a catch at the wicket', 'narrowly escaped being stumped', and was missed off 'a ridiculously easy chance to Juniper at deep mid-off', before finally he 'fell to a beauty from Greenfield'. By the end of the season Abel was recognized as the best of the colts who had emerged from the April trials, but in five innings he had made only 17 runs. 'Disappointing were my feelings as the result of my debut in first-class cricket. I have a most vivid recollection of my only desire at the end of my innings in those days – to run home and hide myself from the public view.'

1882 started rather better. In a series of Surrey Colts matches during the first three weeks of May he turned in some good performances, including 65 against Fourteen of Nunhead Clubs followed the next day by 98 against Malden District. He was then

picked for the first match of the season – against the Australians and
noteworthy for being attended by John Ruskin, who apparently
remarked to 'The Old Buffer', after cover-point had run out a
batsman, that he found cricket to be 'envious and unkindly, for no
sooner has a batsman achieved a noble blow than someone is alert to
obstruct his effort and despoil him of his reward.' The start of the
match was delayed because of rain, but Shuter won the toss for
Surrey and, as Abel soon heard, decided to bat: 'I was in the
players' room when a message came to me from Mr Shuter to get
my pads on and go in first to face the "demon" Spofforth and Boyle
on a sticky wicket.' He got to 11 before a shooter from Spofforth
spreadeagled his stumps. He opened again in the second innings
and put Garrett to square leg for three. He then faced Boyle,
whereupon 'Spofforth came in from point to within about three
yards of my bat, remarking, "I think this will do for the young
'un." ' And, 'feeling quite paralysed, I simply poked the first ball
from Boyle gently into his waiting hands.' The next match was at
Trent Bridge and Abel with a patient 31 was second top scorer in the
first innings. From that point, though, his season declined into a
state of near terminal disaster as far as his career was concerned.
His next twenty-three first-class innings brought him only 131 runs,
including eight ducks; and by the very end of the season, after
inexorably slipping down the batting order, he was no longer in the
eleven. Almost the only bright spot came at the tail-end of the
return match with Notts, when as last man he 'gave unexpected
trouble' and with an obdurate 8 delayed the inevitable innings
defeat before he was out 'in attempting a short run'. And a few days
earlier, playing for the Club and Ground versus South Wales, he
made 51 out of 73 scored while at the wicket. But in general it had
been a demoralizing first full season in county cricket. 'Of little use
except in the field' was *Lillywhite*'s stern verdict on Abel's value to
Surrey that year, and the figures allow no argument.

What probably saved his skin at this point was a remarkably
perceptive report presented in November 1882 by a small sub-
committee (including Burbidge) to the main Surrey committee. Its
subject was the problem of developing young professional talent,
in particular batsmen, and it strongly reiterated Gale's point that
aspiring young professional batsmen had the odds heavily loaded
against them because the only occasions that the amateurs regularly

stood down was when the oppositon bowling was likely to be at its most difficult, in other words in the out-matches against the northern counties. And the report continued:

Professionals are not made cricketers in a season. An amateur most possibly begins his cricket education from the time he can hold a bat. Most certainly he ought to have finished it, at least the theoretical part of it (if a public school boy) by the time he is eighteen. He has cricket drummed into him for years and years, and if not fairly proficient at that age he never will be. Now a professional cricketer seldom if ever commences his real cricketing education until he is past that age. True he may have played on his village green and be even considered a great man there, but what a figure he cuts when he comes against really good bowling? Many of his faults have to be eradicated; in fact you have only the bare raw material to work upon, however good it may be.

Finally, after noting that 'the counties which are at the top of the tree year after year are those which depend almost entirely upon their players' and recalling Surrey's own palmy days when she did likewise, the report made its main concrete recommendation, which was that, in addition to more Club and Ground matches, there should be fixtures against the better non-first-class counties, such as Leicestershire, Derbyshire, Somerset, Essex, Hertfordshire and Hampshire. For if this policy was adopted, 'it would give the young professionals a chance of earning fair remuneration and could give them practice against bowling which, although not quite up to the force of the leading counties, would nevertheless be strong enough to test them thoroughly; and if they could prove themselves good enough to hold their own against this bowling we might be pretty confident that they would train on for better things.' The report proved a turning-point: Surrey markedly expanded their fixture list for 1883 and, in accordance with the general theme of patience, the reputedly twenty-three-year-old Abel was given a further opportunity to train on.

The rewards were instant. In the first match of the 1883 season, at Trent Bridge, his 45 was the top score of the contest; while the following week, at home to Hampshire in one of the new non-first-class fixtures, he made 83 out of Surrey's gargantuan 650, the highest score to date in a match between counties. These two performances gave Abel the platform he needed. 'For the first time I felt I had justified my place,' he later recalled about the innings against Notts. Over the rest of the season and the following two years he steadily consolidated his position in the Surrey eleven, averaging about 20 and achieving some creditable performances. The first one to earn him the accolade of a demonstration by the Oval crowd in front of the pavilion at the end of a day's play came in fact later in 1883, when his 60 helped Surrey to achieve on the last afternoon an improbable draw with Yorkshire. Two years later, at Cheltenham, he carried his bat for the first time with an undefeated 88 in three and three-quarter hours. In 1885, indeed, he was a model of steadiness, making only one duck and his batting being described by *Wisden* as 'consistently good throughout'. By this time, moreover, he was usually opening the innings, a position that suited his essentially patient, methodical style.

But it was 1886 that finally saw the great leap forward, as Abel emerged as one of the leading professional cricketers in the country, scoring 1,221 runs at an average of 29.71 and making his debut in the Gentlemen versus Players fixture. Two of his innings for Surrey that year stood out. In the first match, starting at the Oval on Easter Monday, his 110 against Gloucestershire was his maiden first-class century. Early on he nearly fell to Grace's well-known deep square leg trap, and twice he was dropped by Gregg at mid-on off W. G., but eventually after almost four hours he reached the coveted landmark. Not surprisingly, 'on returning to the players' room he was loudly applauded'. Still more momentous for Abel, though, must have been his innings in July for Surrey against the Australians. At the end of the first day Surrey were 39 for 1 in reply to the Australians' 185, with Abel 18 not out. The second day was astonishing: only two wickets fell, the total advanced to 427, and Abel batted right through to finish on 144 not out. He played the part of sheet-anchor to perfection, putting on 135 with W. W. Read and then an undefeated 241 with Maurice Read, who himself finished that day on 156 not out. According to the *Sportsman*, 'His display was almost faultless, the only blemishes that can be discovered being a possible chance to Spofforth at short leg with his score at 27, the ball coming very low down, and a difficult one to Jarvis at the wicket shortly before lunch.' He reached his century at about four o'clock and 'the score continued to rise steadily', though (in what was an era still without tea intervals) he 'was gradually "fagging", and with the score at 386 Maurice Read gave his partner the "go by".' At half past six 'the crowd literally mobbed the two batsmen on their return to the dressing room and cheered them vociferously'. The following morning Abel was caught at short mid-on off Giffen without any addition to the total, but Surrey finally made 501 and then bowled out the Australians to win by an innings and 203 runs. It was a comprehensive victory, not only marking Abel's coming of age as a top-class batsman, but also ushering in the greatest years of success the county was to know until the 1950s.

Surrey's playing record had, in fact, been gradually improving since 1883, so that by June 1886 *The Times* was able to remark that 'it is many years since a southern county has been represented by so powerful a team as that which Surrey can now place in the field'. In 1886 itself Notts just pipped Surrey for the title of champion county, but the honour then went to Surrey in 1887, 1888, 1890, 1891 and 1892, while in 1889 it was tied for with Lancashire and Notts. 1893 was an unsuccessful season, but Surrey then won the title again in 1894, 1895 and 1899, before the sad decline of the early 1900s set in.

In the course of Surrey *v* Yorkshire at the Oval, 1892

In other words, Surrey won or shared in the title no less than nine times during Abel's career. The captain of the side up to 1893 was John Shuter, who was succeeded from 1894 to 1899 by K. J. Key; but in playing terms the side's most important amateur during these years of success was undoubtedly W. W. Read, who played from 1873 to 1897 and was described by E. V. B. Christian in 1902 as 'probably the greatest Surrey batsman after Jupp until Abel's powers reached maturity'. But as Burbidge had foretold, it was to their professionals that Surrey owed the greater portion. Not all were indigenous: Harry Wood came from Kent and Bill Lockwood from Nottinghamshire, while Tom Hayward originally learnt his cricket on Parker's Piece, Cambridge. Indeed, most of the professionals, including of course Abel, had served their early cricketing apprenticeship on similar areas of inevitably fairly rough open ground: amongst others George Lohmann on Wandsworth Common, William Brockwell on Ham Common, F. C. Holland in Battersea Park, Tom Richardson on Mitcham Common, and Maurice Read on the green at Thames Ditton.

The greatest of all these professionals was Lohmann, whose career was at a relatively early age first stunted and then destroyed by tuberculosis. As a superb medium-fast bowler, nerveless batsman, and unrivalled close fielder he was beloved by the Surrey crowd until his health began to break in the early to mid 1890s. His background was unusual in that his father was a stockbroker who had 'failed' soon after Lohmann's birth, probably in the Overend Gurney crash of 1866. Perhaps the fact that he was caught between two worlds accounts for Shuter's retrospective remark about Lohmann that 'his chief fault lay in the fact that he felt too keenly failures by other members of the eleven in the field'. But whatever the justice of this, there is no denying that, even more than Abel, W. W. Read, or Tom Richardson, he was *the* Surrey cricketer in the silver age of Surrey cricket.

Sizeable (and mostly standing) crowds watched this cricket, averaging around 15,000 for home matches that often lasted only two days. The Oval crowd of the period had the reputation, especially amongst northern sporting journalists, for extreme partisanship. In the early 1880s its particular target was Crossland, the Lancashire fast bowler with an action of doubtful legitimacy. In 1882 there was much loud criticism from the ring as he took 6 for 30;

the following year, after he had again devastated the Surrey batting and been mobbed by an angry crowd on his way back to the players' room, Hornby as a protest delayed for a considerable time the start of the Lancashire innings; and in 1884 the attendance on the first day of the fixture was 'strengthened from a rumour that had gained general credence that Crossland's appearance might be the means of bringing about some ebullition of feeling', but at the last moment he did not play. Certainly it was not always a sporting crowd. When in 1895 Webbe of Middlesex was bowled by Richardson with a no-ball, 'almost every subsequent delivery which he received was greeted with shouts of "no-ball"', and 'the same cry greeted him on his retirement to the pavilion'. Yet on the whole the Oval crowd seems to have been remarkably generous in its appreciation of Surrey's opponents, as in 1890 when, at the end of both the Yorkshire and Kent matches, it 'cheered the victors with as much gusto as if their own men had won'. Nor did the crowd particularly relish watching Surrey steamroller minor opponents, a not infrequent occurrence in these years. Thus, during the Leicestershire match of 1897:

The first hour or so after the interval was mainly devoted to the hitting of fours, each of which evoked rather less enthusiasm than the one preceding, as the spectators became tired of witnessing the ball speed past the fieldsmen to the boundary. The downfall of Abel's wicket at 271, and the hoisting of three figures to Hayward's credit shortly afterwards, were the next incidents to arouse the spectators to manifestations of approval, the cheering becoming louder still when at 324 Hayward was at last disposed of.

The crowd could also be cruel to its own men, as when in 1889 Shuter was reported as being 'very much annoyed' at the way the spectators had 'set about chaffing Key' for his lack of agility in the field. What form in general their abuse took is not known, but in the committee minutes for 1898 there is a passing reference to how, since the club had started employing plain clothes men, seven people had been ejected from the ground 'for use of improper language'.

When the police were really needed, though, was for the Notts match, which from 1882 invariably began on the August Bank

Holiday. Thus for the fixture in 1889, it was 'resolved that fifty police constables with officers and three mounted police be engaged'. The size of the crowds, especially on the first day in the years when Notts were challenging Surrey for the title, was explanation enough: thus 24,450 on the Monday in 1887, 20,836 in 1889, and in 1892 no less than 30,760, which, followed by the crowds on the next two days, took the total for the match to 63,763, then a record paying attendance for a county fixture. On Bank Holiday Monday in 1887 resumption of play after lunch was delayed for some time:

> The spectators had swarmed over the ground, and the efforts of a handful of policemen to get them back to the boundary proved altogether futile. A ring was made some forty yards within the prescribed limit, and here spectators about ten deep placed themselves upon the grass. Nothing could persuade them to retire, and eventually a battle between those behind and the intruders took place. The former dug up sods and hurled them at the ones in front, and not content with this ginger-beer bottles and stones were brought into play, and for about half an hour a fierce war raged between the parties.

On the corresponding day in succeeding years the crowd was rather more orderly: thus in 1888 ' the demeanour was one of rapt attention', while in 1891 'any little incident at all allied to humour – a mistake in the field or an error in batting – was never passed over by a large section of the spectators'. A correspondent for the *Daily Graphic*, who had been sent to the first day of the historic 1892 match, did his best to capture the atmosphere:

> For nearly six hours this assemblage of 30,000 people sat or stood, doggedly watching every ball that was bowled, every stroke that was made, stolidly smoking all the while and all together. The Oval is the Newmarket of cricket. At other grounds the turf is brightened by a bordering of pretty frocks, the applause relieved by feminine chatter; but at the Oval the crowd is black, black thickly peppered with the pink of faces; and the batsman who smites the bowler for four or the bowler who smites the wicket of the batsman is applauded in a roar.

The doyen of the Oval crowd was Albert Craig, commonly known as the Surrey Poet. A Yorkshireman, he was born in 1850, originally worked as a post office clerk in Huddersfield, and apparently came down to London in 1883 on an impulse, claiming afterwards that he had never got round to using the return half of his rail ticket. He derived his income from his instant celebration in verse of sporting events and, though best known at the Oval, he worked his passage round all the major grounds in the South of England. 'A tall, grey, hatless mountebank,' is how Travers remembered him, 'selling at a penny a sheet the ill-copper-plated samples of his doggerel.' His great catch-phrase was 'Wait till we meet you again', and there is no doubt that he was an immensely popular figure with his fellow-Ovalites, especially as he often seems to have had a hotline to the news and would then walk round the boundary telling the crowd who had won the toss or when play would be restarting. The actual quality of the verses that he sold was at best mediocre, typified by the ending of one as recalled by Travers:

> Harry Wood has a story I've oft heard him tell,
> That the sparrows themselves know when Bobby does well:
> They take a front seat 'mid the cricketing throng
> And when Bob gets his cent'ry they burst into song.

That Craig was a personal friend of Abel as well as his most eloquent admirer was clearly shown after his death (despite a get-well message from the King) in 1909. Abel not only attended Craig's funeral and sent a floral tribute to his pauper's grave at Nunhead Cemetery, but also helped to prepare for publication the following year a collection of Craig's verses in aid of his widow. Craig, who had once invested £200 in a Yorkshire mill company that failed, told Abel shortly before his death that, contrary to popular opinion, he had in fact 'never gained more than a modest competency from the sale of his poems'. And Abel added in his brief but warm introduction to the collection: 'I knew Craig – or Bert, as he was to me – better than most people. He was a difficult man to get to know, but when you got below the surface, you found him to be a deep and earnest thinker, not only on the problems of this life but on those of the next.'

Abel, of course, was an integral part of the events that Craig

chronicled, though during the meridian seasons of 1887 to 1892 it
would be fair to say that Surrey won their titles largely on the
strength of irresistible bowling and that Abel was one of the county's
leading batsmen rather than, as he later became, the undisputed
number one. Various landmarks stand out during this middle phase
of his career for Surrey. In 1888, in the summer between two winter
tours, he achieved the distinction of being the top professional
batsman of the season and in consequence made his debut for
England. His highest score of that year was 160 versus Cambridge
University, but probably his most valuable innings for Surrey was
his 77 out of a total of 237 that helped to win the invariably crucial
match at Trent Bridge. 1890 saw a different type of landmark: only
a few months after being chosen as one of *Wisden*'s 'Nine Great
Batsmen of the Year', he was for the only time in the main body of
his career dropped from the Surrey eleven purely on account of bad
form, unrelated to any physical ailments. The match was away to
Sussex and his place was taken by R. N. Douglas, 'the young
Cantab', who made 17. But Abel was quickly back and soon made
centuries in successive innings against Middlesex and Lancashire.
The following year, ironically versus Sussex at Brighton, he made
his highest score to date:

> I ought to have got my first 200 in this match. Brockwell had
> just come in and told me my score was 198. My wife had just
> reached the ground. Humphreys sent me up one of his under-
> hand lobs, which I jumped in to drive for the odd two, with the
> natural pride of making my first 200 in the presence of my
> wife. I missed the ball, and before I could get back into my
> ground, Butt had my stumps down. I then discovered I had
> made 197, and not 198. Had I known this, I should not have hit
> out, as three off Humphreys wanted a lot of getting, owing to
> the placing of his field well on the boundary.

Abel batted soundly throughout 1891 and *Wisden* noted how 'it
was his consistently good scoring more than any one long innings
that made him so invaluable to the team'. If, though, one had to
choose a single match that best epitomized the role that Abel played
for Surrey during these championship years, it would perhaps be
the one versus Middlesex at the Oval in 1889, the one in fact when

he declined to walk. Surrey won the toss and as usual he opened
with Shuter. 'The first hour's play produced but 50 runs, and to this
number Abel contributed a fifth share only.' He then started to
score a bit more freely and eventually was third out at 239, having
batted three hours and twenty-five minutes for his 85. He was
'loudly cheered for his capital display', especially as 'towards the
close of his innings he played a ball extremely hard on to his left
foot, which caused him great pain to the end'. But as the report so
eloquently put it, 'by this time the Middlesex bowling was about
played out'. Surrey finally reached 507, with W. W. Read making a
century, and then mopped up the opposition for 236 and 197 to win
by an innings, Abel taking three catches. He would not perhaps
have got the man of the match award, but he was widely recognized
as an indispensable member of the side.

Home to Middlesex was a favourite fixture, for one of his first
innings in 1894 after the semi-hiatus of the previous season was a
superb 136 not out against them. 'Patiently our favourite plays/
Bowlers change, but still he stays,' the Poet proclaimed, as Abel
carried his bat in a total of 300. The innings marked the beginning of
Abel's great period, during which Surrey's bowling was no longer
always the prime force it had been and the little man's ability to
accumulate seemingly at will became increasingly important to the
county's fortunes. As Abel himself recalled of the 1894 season and
its aftermath:

My aggregate of 1,447 in all first-class matches was my best to
that date, and from having been regarded, in many quarters,
as at the close of my cricket career, in the language of the press
I commenced in 1895 'to reel off' my 2,000 runs and more each
season, and to play better in middle age than at any period of
my career.

Apart from, of course, improved batting on Abel's part, two
things helped to account for this remarkable quantitative take-off.
The first was the expansion of the first-class county programme:
Somerset had already in 1891 attained first-class status and were
joined in 1894 by Derbyshire (who had been demoted in 1888),
Essex, Leicestershire and Warwickshire, followed by Hampshire
in 1895 and Worcestershire in 1899. The second factor was the

general improvement towards the end of the century in the quality
of wickets, an improvement that prompted Shuter to remark in
1902 that whereas in his day 'a total of 300 was pretty sure of being
a winning score, at the present time a side is by no means safe even
with a score of 500'. Figures indeed deceive, but what matters
are relative performances, in other words how at any one time a
cricketer performs relative to his contemporaries. And as *Wisden*
noted in its summary of Surrey's cricket in 1898, 'among a splendid
array of run-getters, Abel, as in several previous years, was the
finest bat'.

Inexorably over these prolific seasons he pushed up his highest
first-class score: 217 versus Essex in 1895; 231 versus Essex in 1896;
250 versus Warwickshire in 1897; and finally 357 not out versus
Somerset in 1899. Then in 1900 his twelve centuries in the season
surpassed Ranji's freshly created record of eleven. He established
the record in a festival match at Hastings, but, as the *Athletic News*
related, the real tension came in the home match with Derbyshire
in which he equalled it:

> The great little man, when 93, put in a series of dervish-like
> turns with his bat in his hand – why, was not clear – and then
> fluked a ball from Ashcroft, which beat him, to the boundary.
> He made a number of indifferent strokes when he got to the
> other end, but the thing was done. No wonder Abel was
> nervous. He is not a young cricketer and is scarcely likely to
> repeat the feat.

The following year he took another of the Prince's records,
surpassing the 3,159 runs that Ranji had scored in 1899. He did so
with fewer centuries (seven) than anyone has ever made in scoring
over 3,000 runs in a season, but again at the last his nerves almost
betrayed him and his cumulative steadiness. 205 not out versus
Middlesex left him only a dozen short when his captain declared:
'Mr Jephson was unaware of this at the time, and I do not know
whether he regretted the closing of our innings more than I did
when the circumstance was brought to his notice.' There then
followed 2 and 0 at home to Leicestershire, and 5 in the first innings
for An England Eleven versus Yorkshire at Hastings, before in a
light-hearted third-day festival atmosphere, with Tunnicliffe opening

Abel's day at the Oval: *v* Middlesex 30 August 1901

the bowling, he squeezed out the final five runs amidst 'a burst of cheering'. Again, it was not at the age of forty-three a feat that he was likely to repeat.

In Abel's time a Surrey season tended to follow a fairly recurrent pattern. Most years the eleven would tone up in May with a series of home matches against the lesser counties. Abel generally did well in these fixtures, for instance in 1884 taking 93 off Essex in the first match of the season and then the following year opening his account with solid scores of 49, 34 and 36 against Essex, Hampshire and Leicestershire respectively; while in 1891, versus the same three counties, he scored 197 runs in four innings in preparation for the sterner tests ahead. But, happily for his career statistics, it was not until after these weaker counties had received first-class status that Abel revealed a penchant for piling up a series of big scores at the Oval in the early weeks of the season. 1896 showed the way, with a sequence of 138 versus Warwicks, 152 versus Leicestershire, and 231 versus Essex. It was remorseless stuff, and in the last of these innings he was apparently 'as steady with his score at 150 as when he had made a third of that number'. He then went to Derby and played on for 2. 1897 saw a similarly flying start: 144 versus Leicestershire, 8 and 95 versus Essex, and 250 versus Warwickshire were rounded off with 5 and 156 from Sussex's bowlers. Before the first of these innings he had had no practice in the middle, but 'from the moment when he cut the first ball of the match for four to the end of his innings, he showed all that easy and vigorous precision which has invariably brought him runs all round the wicket'. In its way 1900 represented an equally formidable start to the season. Although missing several matches through injuring his hand soon after he had scored 65 against London County in a bitterly cold mid-April encounter, he then in four successive fixtures at the Oval made 221 against Worcestershire, 68 and 4 against Essex, 165 and 12 against Sussex, and 104 against Gloucestershire.

Indeed, it was at the Oval in May that he achieved in 1899 his record score, though it was late May and he had made by his standards only a moderate start to the season. The opponents were Somerset, who were handicapped by the absence of their slow bowler Tyler, who had a strain, and the fact that Woods was only able to bowl sixteen overs during the innings. Surrey batted first and just over eight and a half hours of cricket later Abel carried out his bat for 357, a score which up to then had only been bettered by MacLaren's 424 against the same hapless opponents. Surrey totalled 811 and 'all through Abel played very seriously and always seemed the complete master of the bowling'. Or, as another report put it less flatteringly, 'He started cautiously, he continued cautiously, and he was playing cautiously when the end of the innings was at last reached.' But, 'needless to say, he came in for a great ovation on returning to the pavilion'. *Cricket* tried to put the achievement in perspective: 'Abel did not show a sign of weakness; he hardly gave a chance; he never tired; and he never hurried. It may be that the bowling was not brilliant, but it takes a great batsman to make nearly 400 runs when it is not absolutely feeble, which it never was.' And the magazine added in its match report: 'The Somersetshire men never lost their equanimity during this long innings, and the last ball was bowled with as much determination as the first.' Certainly they needed all the equanimity they could muster, especially the wicket-keeper, who missed the only two chances Abel gave, stumping ones when he had made 224 and 237. While at cover-point for Somerset in that match was Captain (later Admiral) Cecil Hickley, who found himself engaged in so many fruitless pursuits that at one stage a man in the crowd shouted, 'Let go your anchor, captain – you'll never catch her.'

The other distinctive feature of the first half of most seasons was the three major northern matches: at Nottingham starting on Whit Monday and then, usually in June and in succession, the away fixtures with Lancashire and Yorkshire. Abel's average in the Trent Bridge match was a reasonably creditable 28.33, and though inevitably he had his bad years – such as being out first ball of the match in 1886 and making 3 and 1 in 1889, and 1 and 0 in 1892, and 6 and 0 in 1901 – in general he followed on well enough there from those encouraging early performances of 1882 and 1883. The year previous to his good performance in 1888 he 'batted with plodding patience' for three hours and forty minutes to make 44 and help Surrey to their first win on the ground since 1870. And in 1891 he twice made top score, 103 and 63 not out, as Surrey defeated their closest rivals of the year by five wickets, with the local paper describing the touching scene following his dismissal in the first innings: 'Such a round of applause as he got when retiring to the pavilion. The little man was quite unnerved, and ran in hot haste away from the plaudits.'

Further north, though, it was a different story. By the end of 1894 Abel after forty-three county innings in Yorkshire and Lancashire was averaging a paltry 16.51, though subsequently some decent scores pulled this average up by the end of his career to a semi-respectable 22.59. In these latter years the contrast with his un-remitting run-making at the Oval could hardly have been greater. In 1900, for instance, five matches at home base had given him an average of 91 before he began his travels with 46 and 19 at Trent Bridge and 23 at Cambridge. Then came the northern tour proper: at Old Trafford on an admittedly bad wicket he was dismissed twice on the first day, being caught and bowled by Briggs for 6 and playing on to Sharp for 16; while at Bramall Lane he was bowled off his foot by Brown for 2 and caught behind off Rhodes for 6. In fact, he did not in general do all that badly at Old Trafford, with several praiseworthy performances on rain-affected wickets and centuries in 1895 and 1898. What he could not do, though, was score runs in Yorkshire: over the years sixty first-class innings (for Surrey and others) played in that county brought him only 1,087 runs, at an average of 18.74. In county championship matches he only managed one century there, at Bradford in 1901, but at least it was a good one. The *Bradford Daily Telegraph* was positively ecstatic about his 125: 'Books of cricket may be written, but to watch the little man is worth the lot. The Yorkshire bowling never seemed so completely in a knot at any previous time this last three years, and you would scarcely have believed it was the best attack in England he was playing so nonchalantly.' But one feels that as far as most York-shiremen were concerned, even the unprejudiced ones, they would by this time have long ceased to believe in the merits of the much-trumpeted 'Bobby'.

Surrey's most attractive home matches tended to be in the second half of the season and one of course was the return with Yorkshire. Despite the personal low-scoring associations, and with the Notts match ruled out of court, Abel chose this fixture for his benefit match in 1895. In playing terms it could have been a happier choice, as Surrey lost by an innings and only managed in the match to total 214 runs, though the beneficiary made 55 of them. 'A grand cheer floated up' as he walked out to open the batting on the first

morning, which may have consoled him a few minutes later as he
found himself being 'badly "stuck up" once or twice' by bumping
balls from Jackson, causing him to 'look sorrowfully at the pitch the
while'. In fact, following rain, the wicket became increasingly
problematic and in the second innings his 23, ending when he
jumped out to drive Wainwright and was bowled, proved to be top
score. Indeed, it was not in general until rather later in the 1890s
that Abel really began to use the home matches of late July and
August to redeem with interest the annual blow to his average
incurred by northern travels. Thus in the last six weeks of the 1898
season, his scores at the Oval included 111 versus Hampshire, 148
and 53 versus Essex, 114 versus Yorkshire, 55 versus Sussex, 219
versus Kent and 135 versus Warwickshire. According to *Wisden*, he
was 'especially delighted' with his century versus Yorkshire, his
first against that county. Or take 1899, when starting on 31 July he
unrolled a sequence at the Oval of 9 and 91 versus Kent, 112 and 29
not out versus Middlesex, 61 versus Notts, 193 versus Yorkshire,
178 versus Lancashire, 167 versus Hampshire and, continuing the
worrying downward trend, 94 versus Warwickshire. The innings
that features in the record books was that played against Yorkshire.
After the visitors had made 704, Surrey at the end of the second day
were 169 for 3, with a 'very quiet' Abel, batting number four, on 42
not out, having already put on 111 with Hayward. The next day,
with no prospect of a positive result to play for, the two just batted;
and with such sureness that, as one reporter put it, 'no separation
looked probable before the millennium'. But a few minutes before
half past five Hayward fell, after putting on 448 with Abel, which is
still a record English partnership for the fourth wicket. And the
spectators, who had grown steadily more sated and unenthusiastic
as the match had gone on, managed to stir themselves sufficiently to
raise a collection of just under £73 for their favourite long-term
occupants of the crease.

On the first Monday of August there began the match that the
Ovalites persistently regarded as 'the big one'. Abel's career record
at home to Notts was steady rather than spectacular, averaging
31.57 in thirty-six innings, but especially during the memorable
seasons of the late 1880s and early 1890s, when Surrey and Notts
were slugging it out for supremacy, he usually did well. In the
second innings in 1889 an opening partnership of 140 with Lockwood

decisively put Surrey in the driving seat; the following year his stand of 61 with Shuter on a treacherous wicket on the first morning had an effect on the match that according to *Wisden* 'it would be difficult to overestimate'; and in 1891, when Surrey won by an innings on another rain-affected wicket, he top-scored with a patient 49 'worthy of his great reputation'. Then in 1892, in front of record crowds, was played the county match of the epoch. On an over-watered wicket Surrey batted first and totalled 129. Abel's 14 in just under an hour – 'batting extremely well, but seemingly unable to get the ball away' – ended when Shacklock removed his off-bail. After Notts had replied with 124, Abel played out the first over of the second innings, leaving W. W. Read (an unusual opening partner) to face the second over. The *Sporting Life* told the unhappy story:

> The Surrey crack played a ball wide of mid-on, and the batsmen easily obtained a single. Read, turning round quickly, started for a second run while the ball was in the fieldsman's hands, and ran down the pitch, while Abel also left his crease two or three yards. Robinson quietly returned the ball to Attewell, and the bowler put the wicket down. Abel seemed under the impression that he had crossed Read, and was himself out, and both men commenced to walk away. As each was apparently desirous of suffering the penalty for the un-fortunate blunder, the umpire was appealed to, and he decided that Read had been run out.

Journalistic opinon was fairly evenly divided about who was to blame, but all were agreed that there was never a second run. Abel then settled down and after almost an hour and a half had reached 28 out of 63 for 3, whereupon: 'Shuter cut a ball to Daft [son of the great Richard Daft] at third man, who did not pick it up at the first attempt. The Surrey captain called Abel for the run; but before the professional could get across Daft had recovered the ball and thrown down the wicket.' And Abel was given out, though one of the fielders later told a reporter that he was 'confident' the umpire had made a mistake. Not surprisingly, Surrey failed to recover from these self-inflicted wounds and eventually succumbed by four wickets.

Subsequent matches were less dramatic, but in Altham's felicitous words, 'The long ascendancy of Nottinghamshire in the "middle ages" had invested that county with a glamour which the darker days that followed could not altogether dull, and their August Bank Holiday meetings with Surrey always filled the Oval to overflowing.' In 1897, for instance, a crowd of over 25,000 watched Abel bat right through the first day to make 211 not out and thereby break a trot of only 27 runs in six innings. 'At no time could it be said that he took Jessopian liberties with the bowling,' but he 'had a great reception at the finish and the crowd in front of the pavilion would not disperse until he had answered to their calls.' The next morning he added only four to his score, but Surrey were in a match-winning position and duly did so by nine wickets. The end was not inappropriate: 'A cut from Abel looked like going to the boundary, and the Notts men were running from the field, but Mason stopped the ball. Abel drew away from the next ball as a boy was passing the screen, but the next he drove to the boundary.'

The final set part of the county season occurred towards the end of August with the western tour. From a playing point of view it was often strangely unsuccessful, though the home double that Gloucestershire and Somerset achieved over Surrey in 1900, with Abel making 83 runs in four innings, was the exception rather than the rule. In the course of the 1890s Somerset turned out to be Surrey's real bogey team and several times at Taunton they humbled their otherwise all-conquering opponents, to the unashamed delight of the rest of the cricketing world. Abel shared fully in this discomfort, failing to make a century in twenty-five first-class innings on what was generally considered one of the best batting wickets and averaging only 25.28. Occasionally he had his moments at Taunton, as in 1901 with accomplished innings of 79 and 93, but much more typical was the match there in 1897, when Surrey could not afford to lose if they were to win the championship. In the final innings, with Hayward unable to bat, they needed 211 to win on an improving wicket. Abel, who had made 1 in the first innings, opened as usual with Brockwell, but with the total on 5 there occurred an incident all too reminiscent of the fateful run-outs in the Notts match five years earlier: 'Abel drove a ball straight to Roe at mid-off, and ran down the pitch. Brockwell was quite unprepared for any such foolish action, but seeing that one must be out, and deeming Abel's the better wicket, he crossed, sacrificing his own.' Abel then 'batted with great care', but at 71 was fourth out, 'bowled off his thigh in trying to place a ball on the leg side', for the second time in the match falling to Tyler. Surrey eventually lost the match by 66 runs and with it went their title hopes.

On the whole both they and Abel did rather better in the county of Graces. His career average at Bristol was 58.80 and at Cheltenham 37.28, while his figure at Clifton of 25.25 masked at least one notable performance, namely his innings there in 1888. Many years later C. H. B. Pridham recorded the story of that innings as it had been related to him by Abel personally soon after the Great War:

> 'At lunchtime I was 96 not out, and well pleased with myself as I walked with the players towards the pavilion, when the Old Man nudged me on the shoulder. "Well played, Bobby," he said. "You'll get your hundred all right! I'll go on myself after lunch, and give you a full pitch to leg."' Abel ate his lunch in happy content. Directly he took guard again he saw with satisfaction that the Old Man had taken the ball, and – what was more – along at once came the promised full-pitch to leg. Obsessed with his score at 96, Bobby hit light-heartedly at it with all his strength; the ball soared away high in the air but alas! it dropped into the eager hands of W. G.'s cunningly placed deep-leg fielder.

Again long after the event, the nephew of the the fielder (J. H. Brain) who took the catch provided in a letter to the *Cricketer* an even more colourful version of this tragi-comic episode, as related to him by his uncle. Abel had apparently finished the second day on 99 not out:

> On the morning of the third day the rain was simply teeming down. Cricket seemed quite impossible, so W. G. said, 'We'll take lunch, and then if play is impossible, we will go out and let Bob make one. It is hard luck he shouldn't get his talent money.' After lunch the rain showed no sign of letting up, so the Gloucestershire team dressed themselves in mackintoshes and took the field. W. G. took the ball and said, 'What'll you

have, Bob?' 'Full toss to leg, Doctor, please,' said Bob. Down it came, and Bob hit it right in the middle of the bat into the middle of the stomach of my uncle Jack, who was fielding very close in at square leg. In sheer fright his arms clasped it, and they all walked in again.

Unfortunately, the newspapers of the day tell, as ever, a soberer story. There no doubt occurred some characteristic by-play on W. G.'s part, but as far as the factual outline goes it seems that at the end of the first day Surrey had made 261 for 7 in reply to Gloucestershire's 39, with Abel on 94, that rain washed out the second day, and that on the final day the only play that took place was during the quarter of an hour before lunch. In that time Abel added two more to his score and then indeed 'Grace pitched one up to Abel on the leg-side, which the latter essayed to hit square, but he did not get well hold of it, and was caught by Mr Brain.' The chances are that he then ate his lunch in less than happy content.

Abel like all batsmen was keenly aware of having his lucky and unlucky grounds. For instance, according to Leveson-Gower, 'He had a curious superstition that he could not make runs on the Canterbury ground.' Granted that he averaged only 16.40 there in ten innings, it was not perhaps such an ill-founded fancy. In fact, Surrey in his time only played twice at Canterbury before the turn of the century, in 1890 and 1891, and in three starts he made a respectable 92 runs. But once he was at the height of his fame it is easy to see why he developed his superstition. In 1900 he was bowled leg-bail by Alec Hearne for 5; while the following year he managed only 0 and 1, both times being dismissed near the end of the day's play, with in the first innings a cut taken close to the ground by third man being adjudged a catch by the square-leg umpire. Another ground where he had the reputation for often failing was Lord's, but though indeed he did have some spectacular failures, especially for the Players, his overall average there of 32.21 was only three runs below his career average as a whole. Several of his innings there for Surrey were very fine, none better than when in 1890, restored to the team, he paved the way for an innings victory by carrying his bat for a chanceless 151.

Yet in the end, as the figures most graphically show, there was no place like home. On English grounds away from the Oval he scored a total of 14,413 runs at an average of 29.35, including twenty-two centuries; whereas at the Oval he amassed 17,359 runs, averaged 42.86, and scored fifty centuries. What really caused such a striking contrast was his rich vein of run-making at the Oval from the mid-1890s: so that having by the end of the 1893 season scored only five centuries on his home ground in the twelve years since his debut, he then from 1894 to 1902 inclusive averaged five per season there. Reporting Surrey's first innings away to Middlesex in 1898, when Abel 'completely at sea' was bowled for 0, the remark of the *Star* that 'it seems a pity that the Oval wicket is not a portable commodity' was no doubt a touch sardonic, but in the circumstances not unreasonable. Certainly it is hard to believe that there have been many batsmen of his standing who have favoured their home turf quite so palpably as he did.

Altham's adjective to describe the wicket that Abel in his great years would have liked to carry about with him was 'adamantine'. There is no doubt that from the mid-1890s it yielded very little even to normally penetrating bowlers, unless of course the rain had been at it. Thus when Abel carried his bat for 136 against Middlesex in 1894, the match marked more than just his transition into prolific middle age, for as the *Sporting Life* noted:

> Several times of recent years, in referring to matches at Kennington Oval, there has been occasion to find fault with the extent to which the wicket has worn in the course of the game, and thus it is the more gratifying to be able to congratulate Apted upon the one prepared for the match under notice.

The theme of the perfect wicket was oft reiterated, as when for instance in 1898 Kent fielded out the first day to an Abel double century: 'With the ball coming at a nice pace from the pitch and rarely rising more than half-stump high, the batsmen had quite an easy time, and the wonder is that in five hours' actual batting the score did not average more than 73 an hour.' And in 1899 Ashley-Cooper in *Cricket* calculated that of the forty-two grounds on which first-class matches had been played that season, the Oval had been the sixth most prolific, averaging 31.19 runs per wicket. Top was Taunton on 35.38 runs, while Trent Bridge, Lord's, and Old

Trafford all came fairly well down, with 26.10, 22.29, and 21.92 respectively.

Sam Apted, as much the key to Abel's fortunes in the late 1890s as Fred Burbidge had been in the early 1880s, had become ground-keeper at the Oval in 1887, having been at Bickley Park and, according to Alcock, 'made it one of the best run-getting grounds in the kingdom'. In his youth he had been a Surrey colt and had also played for several clubs, including, he told an interviewer in 1896, Southwark Park: 'I believe that my highest score was 98, in a match in which Abel made 97. We were in together, and out within a ball or two of each other.' In the same interview Apted said something about his methods:

> For some years we have used, for the centre of the ground, marl from Radcliffe, in Nottinghamshire. After it has been sifted very fine, it is mixed in the proportion of one bushel of marl to three of well-sifted loam. This mixture is put over the ground with very great care, so as just to make a covering. When this is washed in, another dressing is put down, and still another after this. The effect is that the top is prevented from breaking and crumbling, and there are no dusty wickets.

Or, in the expressive words of the minutes of the ground committee in October 1895, it was 'resolved to order a truck load of marl'. But there was rather more to Apted's methods than this, as is shown by a defensive letter that he wrote to the main committee in 1901 in the context of the MCC proposing to legislate that in future pitches were only to be watered and rolled:

> I found about seven years ago that the wickets had a tendency to break up, so I tried to find something that I could use to stop this, and after trying several things I found that a mixture of yellow clay and cow manure put on in a liquid form while preparing the wickets brought about the desired result, that was to ensure the wickets lasting three days. I am afraid if we have to stop using this mixture it will have a deteriorating result on the wickets, for the conditions have entirely changed since I have been on the Oval. We get more closed in every year. The vast extension of buildings on our west and

south-west side of the ground; breweries and factories have increased and thrown off vapours that are very injurious to the grass; then the large gasometers on the north-east side and our pavilion shut us in and prevent the sun getting free access to the ground. When I found that by putting on the clay and cow manure (which I contend is not artificial) I quite hoped I had brought about a state of things desired by everybody connected with cricket.

It seems that he was allowed to persist with his patent mixture, to the benefit of another generation of batsmen after Abel. In his autobiography Fred Root recalled playing at the Oval for the first time, shortly before the war, and how he had arrived there at five in the morning just as Apted was unlocking the gate: 'I saw how wickets were doctored to perfection and was initiated into the secret of Apted's dope, which transformed a natural stretch of turf into the most perfect of cricket wickets in the space of a few hours.' And as he might well have added, it was enough to make a man take to leg-theory.

The MCC's criticism of artificial wickets was part of a fairly wide-spread feeling around the turn of the century among the higher echelons that there was something wrong with the game. The prevailing analysis ran somewhat to the effect that there were too many professional batsmen batting too slowly on too many over-prepared pitches, resulting inevitably in a plethora of drawn matches. Surrey's cricket was often cited as a case in point and, as their great bowlers of the early to mid-1890s began to fade, internal events there reflected a clear sense of unease. In 1898, when Surrey came fourth and drew four more matches than they had ever drawn before in a season, *The Times* noted that 'the regret was often expressed among the general body of members that some of the leading amateurs of the day should have been allowed to drift away from the county'. Then in 1899 (even though Surrey won the championship) the storm broke: Key after five years resigned the captaincy because of differences with the match committee over how many amateurs should be included in the team. And the following March the President, Sir Richard Webster, issued a firm directive to the match committee: 'Desirable as it is that the county should always be at the front in county cricket, I certainly do not consider that the championship should be the only object. I should like, if possible, to arrange matters in the future so that at least three places in the eleven in all ordinary county matches should be filled by amateurs.' This policy seems subsequently to have been implemented, to judge by the bitter-sweet Annual Report issued in April 1902: 'The committee regret that they are unable to congratulate the members of the club upon the result of last season's Surrey cricket,' but 'are glad to record that an unusually large number of amateurs played for the county.' Recent results were indeed no cause for congratulation, in that having come seventh equal in 1900 (their lowest position since 1882) Surrey in 1901 managed only a slight improvement to finish sixth. In 1902 they came fourth, but D. L. A. Jephson, captain after Key, then resigned and the rot really set in. Captain in 1903 was the inexperienced L. Walker and the county finished a miserable eleventh, a position they then equalled in 1904 under a series of different captains, with no official appointment being made. In this unsettling context of drift and confusion Abel played out his final seasons for Surrey: the professionals in their room must often have wondered what was going on.

1902 was a wet summer and most remembered for its compelling series of Test matches, but it was also Abel's last full county season. This time there was no monster haul of runs in the early weeks at the Oval, but three matches played there on rain-affected wickets during the first half of the season earned him notable plaudits from *Wisden*: against Essex, though 'repeatedly in difficulties' early on, 'the feat of making 101 was a remarkable one, even for so famous a batsman'; soon afterwards the Australians ran through Surrey twice on the final day, but in each innings Abel made top score, 'overcoming the difficulties against which he had to contend in masterly fashion'; and in June, versus Sussex, he carried his bat for 151 out of 263, ' a remarkably fine innings' in which he was 'rarely or never at fault, despite the fact that the wicket afforded the bowlers some assistance'. The big northern matches were, as usual, less satisfactory: 16 and 28 not out at Trent Bridge; 6 and 13 on a perfect wicket at Old Trafford, being out both times to Barnes, who 'for once was seen in his Australian form'; and at Headingley 7 in the first innings in very poor light, followed in the second by top scoring with 20 out of a dismal total of 72. In fact, the bogey fixtures retained their hold, for 5 in each innings at Canterbury was merely the precursor to being dismissed twice on the first day at Taunton, for 33 and 12, as Surrey slid to their familiar defeat. But he did make up for some previous failures at Leyton, with a magnificent 150 out of a total of 262, and he also made a profitable first visit to Glossop (87 not out) and return visit to Worcester (104), where he had done consistently well since it had come on the county circuit three years previously. This was also the year that for the first time Surrey played their away fixture with Sussex at Hastings, with the match producing 1,427 runs and Abel's share amounting to a respectable 179. The home contests against Yorkshire, Notts, and Lancashire saw nothing special for dedicated Abel-watchers, but he then rounded off his county season at the Oval with a hundred dead against Middlesex, 'a slow and extremely dull innings' compiled in just under five hours, and a much more sparkling 171 versus Warwickshire, made out of 301 while he was at the wicket. In this latter innings his batting 'dwarfed everything' and, as *The Times* rather tartly put it, 'went to show that he could at times play a forcing game to advantage'. It was a pleasurable end to a county season in which he had scored 1,570 championship runs at an average of 47.57 and once more topped the Surrey batting averages, this time by no less than 15 runs. Or, to quote the unadorned prose of *Wisden* again, 'He was as great a batsman as ever.'

In the winter his eyes started to give him renewed trouble. The problem failed to clear, until in March 1903 the committee sent him to Ventnor, where, accompanied by the Surrey scorer Fred Boyington, he gradually improved over the course of six weeks. He missed the early matches of the season, but on 27 May played for the Club and Ground versus Guy's Hospital at Honor Oak Park and top scored with 90, five more than Hobbs. The next day he was in the team for the home match with Gloucestershire, but according to Ashley-Cooper, writing in *Cricket* later in the season, 'When asked to play he candidly confessed that he did not consider himself in a fit condition to do so, and it was only after considerable pressure from the committee that he consented to take the field.' Predictably, on taking the field he 'came in for a rare ovation'; and when it was Surrey's turn to bat his 34 was top score. Surrey won the match by four wickets, inspiring a cockney verse to be sent to the *Athletic News* on the hopeful theme that 'the nawsty toime is pawst' because

'Bobby's back'. It proved a false dawn: despite making 61 in the next match at Trent Bridge, he never really got going during June and, after eleven innings had yielded only 119 runs, was out of the team by the middle of July. The nadir came at Chesterfield, where in the first innings, with Bestwick early on 'bowling at a rare speed', he 'completely lost sight of a yorker, which forced back the middle stump'. The *Derbyshire Times* gave a still more graphic description of the second innings, as he again faced up to Bestwick:

> For three overs Abel strove earnestly to escape the dreaded pair. He had one fine cut beautifully fielded at point, and was probably happier when he at length got a turn to oppose the slower bowler [Hulme], but he spooned the third ball he received up to point, and for the third time in his long career bagged the spectacles.

The other two occasions had been in 1887 at Hastings, for the South versus the North, and in 1897 at Southampton, but neither time had he been in quite such need of runs as he was now.

The rest of his season after being dropped was a prolonged anti-climax. From 10 July to the end of August he played in a series of away-day matches for the Club and Ground, at places like Haslemere, Leatherhead, and Redhill, scoring 627 runs at an average of 31.35. His performances steadily got better, and by report his eyesight also, so that towards the end of August there was talk that he would be playing in the home match that Middlesex needed to win in order to take the title. But he did not play, Middlesex won the match, and on 2 September the papers published a statement by the Surrey club:

> There seems a sort of idea still that the committee are not desirous of availing themselves of the valuable services of Robert Abel. Perhaps the following extract from the committee's minutes may set the matter once and for all at rest: 'The Hon. Secretary reported that in reply to the match committee that Abel should play in the match against Middlesex, he had seen Abel, and Abel had said he did not feel equal to playing county cricket during the present season.'

As more than one paper remarked in their reviews of the season, the dropping out of Abel from the Surrey eleven, coming so soon after the suicide of Arthur Shrewsbury, unmistakably marked the end of an era in professional batting.

1904 saw a slight return, but then the final fade. Critchett reported to the committee in February that 'His sight is much clearer than it was last year, and if he is careful with his diet and in avoiding draughts I have every hope that in the coming season he may make many fine scores for Surrey.' Wearing glasses, he played in the first match of the season and 'in "big barnacles" looked a quaint little object', though he let it be known that he wore the glasses more as protectors than sight-assisters. Nor was this the only innovation at the start of his last season. The *Daily Mail* commissioned one representative of each county to send a few daily observations on matches in progress. Mostly the paper employed amateurs, but Abel was chosen to represent 'the Surrey point of view'. His reports usually proved to be brief and conventional – full of phrases like 'they played a fine game, and so did we' – though after a first day in which Surrey had made 409 for 7, he ended laconically, 'Cambridge don't want rain.'

As a batsman he again began promisingly, with 170 runs in four innings against London County, but then again fell away. The final visits to the big northern grounds were all disastrous. At Trent Bridge he was caught at third man for 3 and then run out for 0 attempting a third run. The following week at Old Trafford he scored only 1 and 0, being out in the first innings, according to J. T. Tyldesley's match report, 'rather funnily': 'In attempting a drive he edged the ball, which hit slip's finger, then his knee-cap, and thence jumped into second slip's hands three yards away.' While at Bradford immediately afterwards his 1 and 2 merely typified two more wretched batting displays by Surrey. He then did not play for the next month, though continued to send in his reports. 'A very slow and dull day's cricket' was the verdict of the Oxford captain W. H. B. Evans after Surrey had batted most of one day to total 399, but, according to Abel, 'There was a good day's cricket at the Oval today, the wicket still being all in favour of the bat.' Then, without spectacles, he reappeared in early July, playing at Blackpool for An England Eleven versus Lancashire and in the first innings scoring 122. Because of the financial need to ensure that there was play on the Saturday the match in the latter stages rather degenerated, with Ward even being allowed to bat in the second innings in place of the injured Poidevin, and was consequently deemed to be not first class; but it was still being played properly at the time of Abel's century, in which, according to Jessop, 'He gave never a chance, nor, indeed, did he make an unsound shot.'

On the strength of this innings he was recalled to the struggling Surrey team and played in most of the county matches until almost the end of the season. On the whole he did not do too badly, sometimes opening, but usually batting at four or five. At Worcester he made 87, while in the next match, at home to Somerset on a rain-affected wicket, he twice achieved top score, with 48 out of 116 and 65 out of 149. He even got 18 and 38 at Canterbury. But it was manifest that his old ability to make really long scores had gone for good. At home to Warwickshire he managed 79, but it took him almost four hours and he became increasingly bogged down as the innings went on, so much so that 'some of the crowd forgot it was "Our Own Bobby" who was batting and jollied the little man.' His last county match at the Oval was versus Sussex. In the first innings he was out for 8 to a 'wonderfully fine catch' by Fry, in the second to a catch by Ranji for 14 as Surrey in a meaningless contest played out time.

There followed, before Abel permanently dropped out of first-class cricket, away matches with Middlesex and Somerset. At Lord's he was caught by Beldam off Trott for 8 and played on to Bosanquet for 2, but it was left to an even happier hunting ground for the last rites to be administered. The first day at Taunton, a Monday, was washed out, but on the second Abel, batting at number four and having 'met with a cordial reception from the small crowd present' on going in, made 9 in half an hour before he was caught behind. Surrey totalled 156, Somerset replied with 69, and Hayward and Davis took Surrey to 64 for 0 at the close of play. On the final day, as Surrey continued their innings on a still somewhat damaged wicket, Abel batted at nine – presumably because he was injured, but unfortunately the local papers do not say. It was not a glorious swansong: almost immediately he was LBW for a duck to the medium-pace bowler Robson, being 'struck somewhat heavily on the knee' and 'walking back limping considerably'. Surrey finally totalled 155, whereupon Somerset scored 243 for 3 to win by seven wickets. According to *Wisden*, 'the wicket rolled out fairly well' for the fourth innings – and this time there was not even Apted's cow dung special to look forward to as an end-of-season average-booster.

Chapter Three

REPRESENTATIVE HONOURS

It is to the Lord's match that cricketers look for the crucial test between Gentlemen and Players. There is an air of importance about the fixture at headquarters by which even the cricketing public are affected. They know the depth of the influence possessed by the Marylebone Club, in whose hands the representative nature of the match reaches a thoroughness that can scarcely be equalled elsewhere.

THIS AFFIDAVIT BY *The Times* in 1891 reminds one that even before Sir Pelham Warner's day people took these things seriously. The county championship had not yet been properly formalized, Test matches between countries were still lower-case affairs, and there was indeed no higher honour in the cricketing world than to represent the Gentlemen or the Players at Lord's. But the 1890s saw a perceptible shift of emphasis, away from those representative forms of cricket that did not fit in with the increasingly staple county-and-international framework of a season. The annual summit at Lord's remained more or less sacrosanct, but as Warner himself noted in his history of the Gentlemen versus Players match, 'With the largely increased county fixture-list and the visits of the Australians, the Oval authorities in the middle-nineties began to experience difficulty in fielding representative sides.' The Surrey executive should have been able to appreciate both sides of the problem, for the committee minutes in 1896 record how, because of Surrey's match with Essex, Abel was not given leave to play for Lord Sheffield's team against the Australians.

Not that representative matches in general were always what they might have been, to take Abel's experiences at the back-end of the 1885 season. His penultimate match was at Harrogate for An England Eleven versus Shaw's Australian Team. 'The team termed England might certainly be strengthened, seeing that nine of the eleven are professionals,' was the opinion of the *Sportsman*. Rain all day on the Saturday prevented a result. The caravan then moved on to Bradford, where Hall's England Eleven, mostly Yorkshiremen and with Abel as the only southern player, took on Shaw's team. As a contest it never recovered from rain delaying the start until the Tuesday. Farce set in at precisely 3.33 on the Wednesday afternoon, when Peate was out hit wicket to conclude the innings of Hall's Eleven, totalling 133 in reply to the opposition's 220. In the words of the *Bradford Daily Telegraph*:

Play was not resumed until 4.35, owing to some dispute as to the way in which Peate struck his wicket, there apparently being a desire on neither side to field again. Peate struck the wicket in a doubtful way, and this had the effect of Hall's Eleven following on. There was a good deal of squabbling and hooting, but no appeal was made as to Peate's action until the players had left the field, and the umpire, it was said, then gave him 'not out'. He and Emmett, however, declined to go to the wickets again. Gunn and Sherwin [both of Hall's Eleven] came out for the defence, but after some delay they went back and their places were taken by Barlow and Abel.

Why Gunn and Sherwin should have gone back is not clear, but certainly their successors were two batsmen happy to bat until the cows came home. Perhaps rightly, for a long time neither of these two matches was deemed first-class, but they have now (including Abel's 48 runs in three innings) entered the statistical pantheon.

Abel nearly made his representative debut in 1884, in June being chosen as twelfth man for the Players of England versus the Australians at Sheffield and then the following month being prevented by illness from playing for An England Eleven (under Hawke's captaincy) against the Australians at Huddersfield. If on both these occasions he was nominated as the token southerner amidst an array of northern professionals, this was not the case when he made his actual representative debut, for Players of the South versus Gentlemen of the South in a fixture staged at the Oval in 1885 specifically for the purpose of giving a boost to southern professionalism. Abel only made 13, but it was an auspicious fixture for him, in that the only other time he played in it, as a testimonial match at Lord's at the end of the 1894 season, he scored 104 and 60.

Inevitably over the years he played for teams got up under a variety of guises: in 1888 for C. I. Thornton's Eleven and for Lord Londesborough's Eleven, in 1889 again for Louis Hall's Eleven, and in 1892, in a benefit match at Trent Bridge for Alfred Shaw, for

Lord Sheffield's Eleven on the tourists' return from Australia. All
sorts of teams gave themselves the label of 'An England Eleven'
and Abel played three times for such teams against the Australians.
The third of these matches was at Eastbourne in 1902, when at the
end of the first day, in reply to the Australians' 154, the English
all-stars were 29 for 5 (Wrathall, Thompson, Troup, Bush, Storer),
with Abel 26 not out and Trumble proving 'almost unplayable'.
Trumble got him the next morning, but he at least had asserted his
right to be in the team. The side known as Staffordshire's Eleven,
that played the Australians at Stoke-on-Trent in 1890, was also a
sort of 'England Eleven', mainly comprising those who had missed
being selected for the concurrent Gentlemen versus Players fixture.
In a low-scoring match Abel made 1 and 0, the immediate prelude
to his being dropped by Surrey.

It would be true to say that in general representative matches
were in Abel's time losing much of their attractive, quirky mid-
Victorian flavour. But if celebrated fixtures like Smokers versus
Non-Smokers were increasingly a thing of the past, he did play
once, in a benefit match at Lord's in 1892, for Married versus
Single, top scoring in the first innings with 54 before being dismissed
by Lohmann. This was probably the only occasion on which he
faced the great bowler in the middle and he did rather better than
in his almost equally rare confrontations with Richardson. Both
meetings with him were at Hastings, both for the Rest of England
versus Mr Stoddart's Australian Eleven: in 1895 Abel was bowled
by his county colleague for 15 in the first innings, before falling to
Peel in the second; and three years later Richardson bowled him
twice, for 5 and 0. But it was of course at Hastings that Abel
established his records of 1900 and 1901. In that first year he came
into the Surrey and Sussex versus Rest of England match neck-and-
neck with Ranji, on eleven centuries each. In the first innings Abel
duly made 107, but Ranji fell at 62 and, as it turned out, had made
his last century of the season. In the eyes of their many thousands of
respective admirers, the rather arbitrary side they were playing for
might have been more appropriately billed as Surrey versus Sussex.

Though fading somewhat towards the end of the century, traditionally a very important domestic representative fixture, over-
shadowed only by Gentlemen versus Players, was that of North
versus South. Abel's overall record for the South, often against the

cream of the country's bowlers, was fairly unimpressive: 852 runs in 40 innings at an average of 21.84. He fared particularly poorly in 1887, with 4 and 6 at Scarborough being followed immediately afterwards by a pair at Hastings. While ten years later, again at Hastings, 'it was greatly hoped that Abel would succeed in making the necessary runs to complete his 2,000, but he was caught and bowled by Hallam for a duck, amid timid expostulations from the crowd.' By contrast 1889 was his *annus mirabilis* in this fixture. At Chichester in June he scored 50 not out in 65 minutes to take the South to an eight-wicket victory; the following month his 55 in the second innings at Old Trafford saw him batting 'in his usual admirable manner, till he had well assured himself of the talent money'; and in September he scored 105 at Scarborough. This last innings seems to have been quite an achievement. It was played on the final day of the match, as the South followed on, and involved an opening partnership of 226 with Grace. 'The wicket, faultless on the previous days, showed signs of wear, and there were one or two nasty spots. Attewell, Shacklock, Peel, and Flowers are about as good a quartette as can be produced, to say nothing of such changes as Ulyett, Chatterton, and Barnes.' And, 'The crowd, which was a large and fashionable one, appreciated to the full the sensational play of the two great batsmen.'

If this, however, was his most notable performance for the South, it was not necessarily the most memorable match in which he played for them. After the North had been beaten in two days at Hastings in 1892, with Abel's 61 as top score for the winners, the two teams met each other on the Saturday in a broomstick match. Fast bowling was not allowed and the sweep shot had not yet been invented. In reply to a total of 184, the South could only manage 79 and 107 for 8, with Abel, batting at a conservative number eight, scoring 13 and 11. W. G. made only 6 in the first innings and, as the *Cricket Field* recounted, did even worse when he took up his broom for the second time:

When he was bowled by the first ball, he claimed that he had a right to a 'trial'. The North team admitted the justice of this claim, and the Doctor proceeded with his innings. Immediately afterwards he was caught, but the crowd constituted themselves umpires and called 'No Ball!' Apparently acting on the principle that the voice of the majority is sacred, W. G. once more took up his position at the wickets, and made a run.

Straightaway, however, he was caught again, and this time he did beat a retreat.

Abel's record for the Players was notably better than for the South: in thirty-four matches against the Gentlemen he scored 2,055 runs at an average of 41.10. His 'mean' performances in the fixture tended to be at Hastings, averaging 42.87 and making one century, but it was at the Oval that, especially in later years, he was really dominant. Nineteen innings there brought him 1,058 runs at an average of 66.12. Not that the sparrows always had cause to burst into song: on his Oval debut for the Players in 1886 he was out to E. M. Grace, the 'Coroner', for a duck, as he 'put one up from the lob bowler in very bad fashion to mid-on'; and in 1895 Fry twice had him caught and bowled, for 3 and 6. But generally, against increasingly unrepresentative sides bereft of fast bowling, he took merciless toll. His first big innings came in 1894 when he carried his bat for 168 out of 363, an innings which 'strongly resembled one of Shrewsbury's famous displays' for the way in which he treated the bowling with uniform respect throughout. The opposition was without Kortright or Woods, and Abel made the utmost of his opportunity after he had been missed twice before reaching 50. Five years later, against another weak attack, his 195 in just under five hours was top score in a total of 647, as he gave 'a perfect display of finished cricket under favourable conditions.' His dismissal was a shade unlucky, with 'a misunderstanding resulting in his falling down on the pitch when he was sent back by Hayward.' And, 'He was accordingly run out, although Mr Jephson, with a pardonable hesitation, did not return the ball as promptly as he might and would have done under ordinary circumstances.'

The following year, 1900, he carried his bat for the second time, with 153 out of 302. The Gentlemen included this time two genuinely fast bowlers, Bradley and Jessop, and early on Abel not only survived 'two dreadful strokes in the slips', but also 'in attempting to score from Jessop he threw his bat a dozen yards away to square leg'. He then settled down and, alone of the Players, mastered the bowling. This match had a curious tailpiece as far as he was concerned, reminiscent of his falling to the wiles of E. M. in 1886.

The Players began their second innings ten minutes before lunch on the second day, as described by the *Sporting Life*:

> Jephson opened the attack with his lobs. Abel hit the first ball to the on for two and from the second was bowled. Abel made no serious attempt to play at the ball, which hit his pads and dribbled between his legs into his wicket. The Surrey professional apparently did not realize his danger until too late, and had the mortification of seeing the bails just shaken off.

A year later the well-known lobster bowled him again, but not before Abel had batted six hours and scored 247. His most dangerous moment came on 78, when he was almost caught at extra mid-off: 'The ball reached More very low down and he caught it, but allowed it to just touch the ground. An appeal was made, but the game decided in Abel's favour.' The bowling was weak – 'so weak that W. G. gave me a long spell!' Warner recalled – and *The Times* waned lyrical about how in addition, 'The weather was oppressive with never a breath of breeze, Abel's batting was prolonged but dull, and there was a humdrum spirit about the whole game.' On the other hand, no one else in the side made over 42 and, as one paper rather nicely put it, '247 is a noble score when one remembers that there are nine ways of getting out to any kind of bowling'. After all, it was hardly Abel's fault if he was denied the chance of another tilt at the fast men.

At Lord's, by stark comparison, life was real and life was earnest, not to say nasty, brutish, and short. Abel's average there for the Players was 26.77, and in twenty-two completed innings he reached 40 only four times. Not surprisingly, his place in the team was not always certain, even if he was having a generally good season. In 1892 he was only included at the last moment in place of the injured Lohmann, while two years later the Marylebone selectors were much criticized on account of Abel's absence from the side immediately after he had carried his bat for the Players at the Oval. And, according to the *Athletic News*, 'The answer from Lord's to the effect that the team was made up before the little Surrey man had made his great innings is not considered very satisfactory.' Abel's really torrid experiences came in the late nineties, at the very time when he was otherwise in his batting prime. In 1897 he was bowled for 5 in the first innings by 'a fine length ball' from Jessop. He 'had never seemed comfortable', had 'made a couple of bad strokes, one being nearly a catch to Grace at point', and the dismissal 'caused no surprise'. In the second innings he made 22 before falling to the medium-paced Cunliffe. The following year was the historic match timed to coincide with W. G.'s fiftieth birthday and it began with Abel and Shrewsbury facing up to some whirlwind bowling from Kortright. 'Both batsmen shaped gingerly enough' and Abel in particular was 'obviously scared once or twice at Kortright's pace'. He reached 7, but 'in playing forward to Kortright, quite lost the ball and had his leg stump bowled down'. The following day he and Shrewsbury tried again in poor light in the last hour of play. Kortright and Woods opened the bowling 'at a tremendous pace', Abel again was 'obviously ill at his ease', and 'having made a single and a beautiful square cut for four had his leg stump sent flying some yards out of the ground', once again by Kortright. Then in 1899, as *Wisden* recorded, he was not originally selected: 'On his form last season there was something rather comical in Abel being a substitute in a Players' Eleven, but the Surrey batsman does not often shine at Lord's, and in this match as it happened he failed dismally.' This time his tormentor was Kent's W. M. Bradley, 'rather a tear-away bowler' and in the middle of a marvellously successful season. In the first innings Bradley had him caught behind for 14, after he had earlier been missed there. 'Abel did not meet him resolutely. Without saying more, one may remark that he drew away slightly from both balls.' And in the second innings Bradley bowled him first ball, lifting the middle stump out of the ground.

This abject sequence was partially redeemed by good performances in 1900 and 1901, before in 1902 Abel made his final appearance for the Players at Lord's. He opened with Tunnicliffe, with Jessop coming in from the Nursery end, and the *Times* critic sharpening his pen:

Partly by luck and partly, perhaps, by a little prudent exercise of judgement in running, Abel was generally found to be playing to Mr Jackson from the other end, but Mr Jessop, bowling very fast, got both Tunnicliffe and Tyldesley dismissed by catches in the slips. Abel's turn came next, as Mr Jessop, bowling his fastest, sent in a good length ball on the leg stump, and not even Abel's correct eye could stop such a ball when the batsman, standing some way towards short leg, played with such a very crooked bat.

He had made only 17, but the Players eventually totalled 444 and won by an innings. Fielding for the Gentlemen at short leg would never be the same again.

Two years were very different. In 1896, after being caught behind off Woods for 4 in the first innings, he and Ward began the Players' second innings just after noon on the second day, following on 152 runs behind. He 'at once settled down to a bright game' and made 94 in just over two hours, being third out at 125. 'Considering the importance of the match, the state of the wicket, and the excellence of the bowling, Abel's performance was simply dazzling in its brilliancy.' All the critics took a similar line to the *Morning Leader* and, as one, agreed that Abel had 'never played better'. 'The little man's batting was beautifully clean, well-timed, and vigorous, and after such a pretty display everyone regretted to see him bowled all over his wicket by what looked like a very simple ball from the "old man".' It was his second 94 in a big match at Lord's in less than a month, so W. G. perhaps felt that a straight one would do it.

Still more notable for Abel was the match in 1900. He went in to bat towards the end of the first day, after the Gentlemen had made 297. Kortright and Jephson opened the bowling, with Abel finding the lobs very tricky, his 'futile endeavours to hit them on the leg side provoking much merriment'. Abel got a couple of boundaries off Kortright, but Jessop then came on and, as he himself later recalled, his first ball 'nearly took away the peak of "Bobby's" cap'. Jessop then hit him two or three times and, in the words of the *Sporting Life*, 'Abel, who was very lame from the effect of Jessop's bowling, was glad to make his way to the other end, where he appeared much more at home with Mason.' At the end of the day the Players had struggled to 66 for 2, with their captain on 29. On the second morning he was still walking lamely and had only added a single before 'Jessop with his fifth ball sent Abel's off stump flying, the stump making two or three complete turns in the air.' His 30 proved to be the top score out of a total of 136. The Gentlemen then made a rapid 339 and at the end of the second day the Players, set 501 to win, were 44 for 1, with the heavily bruised Abel holding himself back. On the final morning, when 'it looked "all Lombard Street to a China orange" against the Players even saving the match', he went out to bat at 81 for 2 and by lunch, in just under two hours at the wicket, had made 94. 'On the game being resumed

Abel seemed certain of his hundred, but he was a little too anxious, and after getting one boundary hit he attempted a big pull off a short-pitched ball from Jessop, and was easily caught at forward short leg.' The score was thus 246 for 3 and through his efforts 'victory for the Players was seen to be possible'. Fry in his column in the *Athletic News* lauded the innings: 'He did little else save hit fours. He played his forward strokes with downright power, and his timing altogether was perfect. It was an absolute pleasure to field out for batting of this sort.' The Players won the match by two wickets, with Brown and Hayward scoring centuries, 'but in the opinion of many good judges', according *Wisden*, Abel 'played the best cricket'. After the previous three years it must have been a sweet day for him, marred only by that fatal but so characteristic nervousness in the nineties.

In the 1897 interview Abel was asked about his two Australian tours: 'Except that the climate is a little trying to an Englishman, I liked cricket in Australia very much, and I greatly enjoyed the tours. I used particularly to appreciate the short interval at half past four for tea after a day's fielding.' The first time he went, in 1887–88, was with G. F. Vernon's team, a tour that suffered from the fact that it was in Australia simultaneously with the perhaps rather stronger party under the auspices of Shaw, Shrewsbury, and Lillywhite. Abel was chosen for the combined team to play Australia in one match, but illness made him drop out. Nor was the tour particularly well organized, to judge by the episode in Adelaide at the end of December. Vernon's team, playing South Australia, had been left with 255 to win and at lunch on the fifth day were 59 for 0, with Abel on 23. Whereupon, despite a prior agreement to play out the match, the game was abandoned and the tourists left for Melbourne, having a (non Test match) date there two days later with Combined Australia.

Abel began the tour well, making 95 in the second innings of the first match, also against South Australia. He showed 'the soundest possible defence' until he 'was within five of the century, when he tried to make the remainder in one hit to the off, but was clean bowled.' A week later, at the very end of the first day's play versus Victoria, he had a fairly harrowing first innings in Melbourne, as reported by the local *Argus*:

Abel scored two from Spofforth's second ball, and then the 'Demon' fairly beat him, but without touching the wicket. Off the last ball of the over Abel should have easily run out in trying for a leg-bye, but Spofforth failed to take the ball, and a great many round the ground, not noticing this, thought Mr Cotter had given an unfair decision. There was some little jeering when Trumble pitched a full toss to Abel, which the little Surrey batsman hit to the fence at square leg, but it quickly changed to cheering when, with the next, he was clean bowled, the ball keeping very low down.

In the next first-class match of the tour, however, Abel took the honours, when against New South Wales at Sydney, and confronting Turner and Ferris for the first time, he batted through the opening day to score 87 out of 263 for 4. But early the next morning he was caught by Alec Bannerman at extra mid-off for 88, provoking the *Sportsman*'s correspondent to write:

Considerable dissatisfaction was expressed by Abel and the Englishmen at the verdict of the local umpire, C. Bannerman, in allowing his brother this catch; and so close was the ball to the ground that no one except those in the field could possibly see whether it touched the turf or the fieldsman's hands first, Alec Bannerman himself being very doubtful about the matter.

He did not again get near to a first-class century during the tour. Certainly not in the match versus Combined Australia, starting on New Year's Eve, when Trott bowled him second ball for a duck with 'a beautiful length leg-break, a great performance on a billiard-table wicket, as it certainly was at that end'. Eventually, after a rather anti-climatic second half of the tour, he totalled 320 runs in first-class matches at an average of 24.80, fourth behind W. W. Read, Peel and Stoddart. While in matches against 'odds' he scored 476 runs at an average of 29.75, with his top score being when he carried his bat for 92 out of 243 in a two-day match against Twenty-Two of Cootamundra. But despite the fact that fate kept on intervening just before he could reach three figures, he still had overall a reasonably fair tour. 'The same reliable cheery little player that he has always shown himself to be in Surrey cricket,' was *Cricket*'s verdict, and so no doubt he was.

The following winter he was one of the rather motley team that under the captaincy of C. Aubrey ('Round the Corner') Smith made the pioneer trip to the Cape. All but two of the matches were played against odds and were therefore not first class. It was a theme that the gossip columnist of the Kimberley-based *Daily Independent* talked to Abel about during the tour: 'The little Surrey bat declared that it is impossible to judge on a batsman's form when there are 15 or 18 in the field. "You see," he said, "where the cricket comes in, is in placing the ball through the fielders and," he continued gloomily, "you can't place a ball through a 22 field. You have just to shut your eyes and hit."' At which point the columnist noted that Abel had in fact shown 'some very pretty placing' during the tour. And the chat went on: ' "If," Abel said, "you played eleven aside you would learn ever so much more about cricket than you can when we play odds." In fact in Abel's opinion cricket is not cricket with odds.' But whatever the odds, Abel was easily the top batsman of the tour, mastering the matted wickets on which many of the matches were played and scoring 1,075 runs at an average of 48.19, double anyone else's aggregate or average. Ulyett, for example, averaged 23.70, and Maurice Read only 17.26. He made two centuries against odds, the first time at Johannesburg versus Fifteen of the Transvaal. Scenes of acclaim followed his eventual dismissal for 114: 'Several spectators rushed out and carried the little batsman on their shoulders, while the band struck up "See the Conquering Hero Comes". Abel was deposited in the centre of the bandstand, and made to bow his acknowledgements to the plaudits of the ladies in the grandstand before he was allowed to retire blushing to the pavilion.' A month later he carried his bat versus Twenty-Two of Grahamstown, for 126 out of 256. Early on, after a quiet start, he 'created a sensation by lifting a leg ball magnificently over the wires on to the telegraph board at the pavilion for six'. At the end of the innings he received a predictably 'royal reception' and later in the day received ten guineas collected from the spectators, 'to which Abel responded with thanks'.

The locals responded to his batting throughout the tour as if to a revelation. Thus, after he had made 36 versus Eighteen of Kimberley, top score in a total of 177:

The gem of the innings was without doubt the batting of Abel. Steady as a rock and sound as a bell, he long remained a thorn in the sides of the bowlers and fielders. No trick took *him* in, and from first to last we do not think he made a single unsound stroke. Even the stroke which proved fatal to him was perfectly sound, but a man happened to be just exactly on the right spot.

The tour was rounded off with two matches against Eleven of South Africa, at Port Elizabeth and Cape Town. These were later deemed to be Test matches, but the standard of the South African team was at best moderate English county. England won the first match by eight wickets and Abel, with 46 and 23 not out, was top scorer in each innings. A fortnight later the pattern was very similar: England won by an innings and Abel's 120 was the highest score. He batted patiently and well-nigh faultlessly for just under five hours, with his only chance, a hard one, being given the ball after he had reached three figures. 'Small in stature, he played perfect defence, but was all alert to take advantage of every loose ball and place it with perfect safety,' was the admiring description in the *Cape Times*. And, as the *Sportsman*'s correspondent wrote in his retrospect on the tour as a whole: 'He has left a reputation behind him in South Africa which is not likely to be surpassed by any cricketer for some time to come. It mattered but little to him if the wicket were fast or slow, the little midget as a rule came out top scorer.'

Three winters later he went with Lord Sheffield's team to Australia on what proved to be his last tour: in later years either he considered the proposed payment inadequate for someone of his age or those selecting the party considered him too old anyway. The team, captained by Grace, was fully representative, apart from the absence of the two leading northern professional batsmen, Gunn and Shrewsbury, who declined the invitation. Abel in his reminiscences reckoned that 'their presence would have steadied a batting list inclined to methods far too free for sustained success on Australian wickets'. On the way out the tourists played two matches: versus Eighteen of Malta (Fleet and Garrison), with Abel's 34 as second highest score; and versus Nineteen of All Ceylon, in which Abel made 10 before he was bowled leg stump by Raffel with, according to the *Ceylon Observer*, 'a splendid break'. This low score at Colombo in fact presaged a series of indifferent perform-ances in the minor engagements of the tour proper, when in eighteen innings against odds he totalled only 310 runs at an average of

18.23. His top score was 50, which he made first against Sixteen of East Melbourne and then, on a matting wicket at Wollengong, against Twenty-Two of Illawara District. Nor, with one famous exception, were his first-class performances any better than steady, though his 388 runs in eleven-a-side matches at an average of 38.80 did place him second only to his captain in the averages. In five state matches his top score was 48, compiled in just under three hours against New South Wales. He tended to get a start, but then failed to go on. Thus, versus Victoria, 'Abel seemed more at home than Grace, and the former's clean, free, and finished play stood out in rather marked contrast to the somewhat laboured and rather faltering efforts of W. G.' But it was Abel who was first out, dismissed by 'one out of the box from McLeod, a fast one which broke back in a way that completely surprised him.' Such also was rather the pattern in two of the three Test matches. In the first, at Melbourne, where Australia won by 54 runs, he played well in both innings, for 32 and 28, but was unable to build. And in the third, at Adelaide, with the series already lost, he made 24 before, facing Trott, he 'ran out, missed him, and was easily stumped by Blackham'. According to the *Australasian*, 'The Australians were much pleased at getting rid of him, as they considered him far more dangerous than Grace.' The reason for this rather flattering estimate lay almost solely in what had happened in the previous Test at Sydney.

Perhaps he was destined to enjoy a triumph, in that the local *Daily Telegraph* noted in one of its match reports on the Second Test that 'the catering for the players and members is in the hands of R. Abel and Co., and has given great satisfaction.' The non-caterer went in with W. G. for the last half hour of the first day, after Australia had made 144, and they took the score to 38 for 0, with Abel on 15. The second day was 'bright, sunny, and genial', the wicket dry, and the attendance almost 24,000. Wickets fell steadily at the other end, but from the start Abel was 'batting beautifully in his smartest and neatest style, his hits being crisp and well-timed.' At lunch he had made 51 out of 126 for 3. Soon afterwards he 'put up a ball softly, and George Giffen started to run to wicket for it, but collided with Peel and could not reach the ball', though according to another account 'it is doubtful whether in any case he could have reached it'; while on 77 he gave from a cut what was possibly a hard chance to Trott at slip. Otherwise he continued to bat with complete authority, so that by the time the last man, Sharpe, came in, he was on 95. He then took twenty minutes to reach the promised land, finally on 97 pushing a short single that led to two overthrows. He had been batting for four and three-quarter hours for his century. 'Having achieved that goal, Bobby again belted, and started to lay on the wood as though he were a Lyons or a Read.' He made his last 32 in forty minutes and put on 71 with Sharpe before the bowler was out. The final England total was 307, with Abel carrying his bat for 132. 'A perfect display' was how George Giffen later described the innings. 'Without taking the slightest risk, he met all the bowling with provoking confidence, and made some beautiful strokes.' Abel himself modestly pointed out in later years that 'the Sydney wicket is the easiest I have ever played on, and if a cricketer cannot make runs on it when it is hard and fast he cannot make runs anywhere.' But by the time that England went in again in this match, needing 230 to win, the wicket, following rain, had undergone a complete transformation. Fifty minutes remained of the fourth day and England lost three wickets for only 11 runs, including Abel's, out for 1. He 'hit vigorously at a leg ball' from George Giffen, skied it to square leg, and Walter Giffen calmly took the catch, amidst shrieks from the ladies' pavilion and the sound of parasols being broken. The innings never recovered from the early disasters and Australia won the match by 72 runs. As the likewise single-initialled Hutton and Boycott were to discover many years later, carrying one's bat in Australia tended to be the mark of playing for a losing side.

Abel made his Test debut at home to Australia in 1888. A fortnight before the First Test, at Lord's, the *Athletic News* asked: 'What are the odds against Abel getting into the England team? Not long, if the modest little Surrey professional keeps his present form. His sole fault is that he "funks" a bit when he gets near his century.' And the paper asked its readers to pick 'A Model England Team'. 1,034 coupons were received, showing Grace and W. W. Read as the two unanimous choices, with Abel coming ninth on 731 votes, well ahead of his county captain's 239. But for the match at Lord's, Shuter was selected and Abel was only reserve; and according to the *Sportsman*, 'quite an outcry was raised at the alleged injustice to the plucky little Surrey professional'. In the end Shuter withdrew, lame, and Abel took his place. On the first day, a Monday, with a crowd of 14,000, rain prevented play until three o'clock, whereupon Australia attacked boldly on a treacherous pitch and reached 116. Abel and W. G. opened for England at a quarter to six, with Abel taking strike from Turner at the Pavilion end. He took a single off the last ball of the over, scored a couple more singles, but then, off the last ball of Ferris' third over, was bowled playing forward. England the next day edged their way diffidently to a total of 53 and Australia then made 60, leaving a target of 124 for victory on a still difficult, drying pitch. Abel again opened with W. G., but 'appeared very unsettled and frequently started for absurd runs'. However, he helped to put on 29 for the first wicket, the second biggest partnership of a remarkable match, before he was 'easily caught at slip' by Bonnor off Ferris for 8. The rest of the batting then collapsed and England, all out for 62, lost by 61 runs. There was a sad ring to *Wisden*'s comment: 'Abel, of whom so much was expected by his friends, probably could not help his play being influenced by his sense of responsibility.' Ironically, it was the type of match in which the more adventurous Shuter might have been likelier to come off.

Abel, however, kept his place for the Second Test at the Oval, one of only two times in his career he played there for England against Australia. A crowd of 17,000 saw Australia on the first day dismissed for 80 on an apparently fast pitch and then England struggle to 46 for 3 by soon after half past four. Abel, demoted in the order, naturally 'met with a warm reception upon walking to the wicket' and over the next hour and fifty minutes, 'playing the bowling with confidence', helped to take the score up to 185 for 5 at stumps. He was not out for a chanceless 65. The following morning, resuming with Sugg, he hit the first ball of the day, from Turner, to the on for 4, added another single, but then 'lost his wicket through venturesomeness', though equally likely it was through nervousness. 'He started for a run from a hit of his partner's and the ball was well fielded by Trott, running from point, who threw the wicket down. It was exceedingly bad fortune for the Surrey professional, who seemed thoroughly set.' The *Sportsman* was less kind than *The Times*: 'It was a great pity that for the sake of a short run, when runs were by no means badly needed, a good wicket should have been sacrificed.' But in the end, from a team point of view, it mattered little, in that England won the match by an innings. The deciding contest of the series was played at Old Trafford. England batted first, with Abel and Grace opening, on what was reckoned to be a heavy pitch. The first four overs and three balls produced no runs on the board, as 'the bowlers appeared to puzzle the batsmen considerably'. At which point Abel was 'altogether beaten by a good ball' from Turner and departed for a duck. From this poor start England recovered to make 172 and win the match, again comprehensively by an innings. In the series Abel had averaged 20.25 and shown himself happiest in familiar surroundings.

It was another eight years before he again faced the Australians in a domestic Test match. In 1890 his poor form during the first half of the season ruled him out of contention, while three years later he was endeavouring to re-establish himself for Surrey after his eye problems. But by the early weeks of the 1896 season his reputation was such that, in the words of the *Athletic News*, 'no England eleven would be considered complete without him'. The First Test that year was at Lord's and began dramatically with Australia collapsing for 53. The England score was 38 for 1, with Stoddart out and Ernest Jones bowling very fast, when Abel joined Grace. It was a dramatic confrontation, as 'Rover' of the *Morning Leader* made clear to his readers: 'I almost feared for Abel against the human catapult from Australia. He is such a little morsel of humanity, and Jones is such a big, swank, sinewy fellow. I had only to see Abel play the first three balls to know that he was as right as right can be.' Or, in the words of the match report in *Cricket*:

> Abel did not seem to like the short ones from Jones, which got up to a level with his nose, but he did not show the least sign of fear, and very soon he had discovered a way of playing them. Once he made a mistake. The ball went perfectly straight to Eady in the slips, who seemed taken by surprise, and after fumbling with it once or twice, let it drop.

It was a bad drop, because Abel, 9 at the time, then started to score fairly freely and after eighty minutes at the crease, with two more wickets down, reached his half century. Meanwhile, off the field of play, there was 'an absence of the quiet and decorum usually characteristic of the Lord's ground', as a record crowd of just under 30,000 battled during the early part of the afternoon for a good view of the proceedings. The ones at the back threw objects,

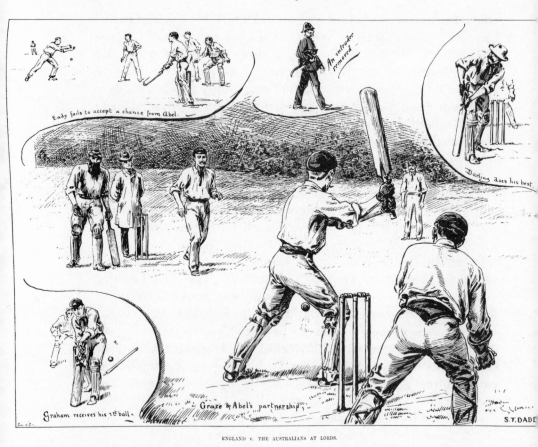

Abel batting: England *v* Australia at Lord's, second Test 1896

'generally a handful of gravel wrapped up in paper', at 'those in front who would stand up', which 'led to a lot of noise, and no little disorder'. Abel must have thought for a moment that he was back at the Oval facing Attewell on Bank Holiday Monday. One result of this was that the crowd encroached about ten to fifteen yards on the field of play and 'many a ball which would ordinarily have been fielded for two, scored four'. The pace of Abel's scoring slackened after he had reached his 50, partly because he had been 'a great deal knocked about, more especially by Eady', so that by the end he was 'very lame, and obviously batting under great difficulty'. The end in fact came when he 'hit right over' a ball from Eady and was bowled middle stump for 94, an innings that had taken him a little over three hours and helped advance the total to 256 for 5. 'A splendid innings' and 'batted with all his exceptional skill' were phrases in the next morning's papers. It was the highest score in a total of 292 and turned out to be his highest in a Test match in England. It also helped win the match for England, by six wickets, though not before, in poor light right at the end of the second day, Abel had fallen to a slip catch off Jones for 4, having opened the innings with W. G. One can be pretty sure that if he had been captaining the Players in similar circumstances, he would not have been found in the middle for those last few minutes.

The Second Test, a victory for Australia at Old Trafford, was from England's point of view dominated by the remarkable performances of Ranji and Richardson. Abel, at number four, batted twice on the second day. In the first innings he put on 81 in seventy-five minutes with Ranji, contributing 26 himself. To quote 'Rover' again: 'We were just beginning to get excited over England's success when Abel – dear little Abel – failed to get over one from McKibbin, and tall Trumble snapped him in the slips.' The second time round he made 13 before falling to 'a brilliant catch at short mid-on' by McKibbin off Giffen. The following month, starting on 10 August, the deciding Test was played at the Oval, and Abel again batted twice on the second day, but there the similarities virtually ended. Most of the first day was lost to rain, but fairly early on the second morning Abel came out to bat at 78 for 2 on a sticky wicket, with the sun out and 'the ball hopping about awkwardly'. He stayed for an hour and a quarter, 'watching the talking ball like a cat watching a mouse' and helping to add 67 runs while five wickets fell. On 18 he gave a difficult caught and bowled chance, but then fell in like manner to Trumble for 26. England totalled 145, Australia replied with 119, and at 12 for 2 Abel was in again. Once more he 'batted with his well-known care' and in particular 'showed all his dogged resistance and exceptional skill in playing Trumble, stopping many balls which would have bowled other batsmen.' After an hour he did fall to Trumble, 'cleverly caught high up right hand by Giffen at short mid-on', but he had made 21 and the score had gone on to 56 for 5. It eventually reached 84 and Australia were then bundled out on the final day for 44, losing the match by 66 runs. Abel had made 47 out of England's

total match aggregate of 229, equal top with Jackson, whose 45 in
the first innings had been scored under appreciably easier conditions.
Hearne, Peel, and Abel were the three players most cheered for
afterwards by the massed crowd in front of the pavilion, with the
local favourite especially 'naturally in great demand'. Whistling
loudly through their fingers and at the top of their voices shouting
for 'Bob-eye', with the accent on the 'eye', the Ovalites were
certainly right not to let the opportunity pass.

In 1899, despite his formidable run-making for Surrey, he did
not play in a single Test. He seems to have been passed over
partly because of his moderate start to the season – with the big one
against Somerset coming just after the team for the First Test had
been selected – but largely because of a widely held belief that he
could not handle fast bowling. The fateful moment was probably
early in May when, representing the South of England against the
Australians on the Crystal Palace ground, he had made only 5
before he 'turned to play Jones to fine leg, but had his wicket
shattered, much to his evident astonishment'. As the summer pro-
gressed he was not without his advocates: 'Abel Emphasizes His
Claims for a Place' was the *Star*'s headline after he had scored 195
against the Gentlemen at the Oval; but then along came Bradley a
few days later at Lord's to provide even stronger evidence for the
other school of thought.

Three years and many runs on, when the Australians were next
over, there was from the start of the season quite a systematic
campaign for Abel's inclusion, though at first without success.
According, for instance, to Ashley-Cooper in *Cricket* after the First
Test: 'The batsmen on the side were too brilliant a set to be reliable,
and a steady bat such as Abel or Shrewsbury to have opened the
innings with MacLaren or Fry was what was required.' Abel's
detractors could now in addition point to his declining speed in
the field, but finally, after some superb performances on difficult
wickets during the first half of the season, he was selected for the
Third Test in place of Fry (who in the end played, because of an
injury to Ranji). The venue could have been happier for Abel's
return to Test cricket: after seventeen innings at Bramall Lane
his average was only 15, his highest score only 36; while as P. C.
Standing subsequently noted about the selection, 'Certain of the
northern critics were unkind enough to hint that it was primarily

due to the "hysterical outcry of a few newspapers in the south".'
Under some pressure, then, Abel opened with MacLaren towards
the end of the first day after Australia had been all out for 194.
But 'the sturdiness of Abel made itself felt'; he began with five
boundaries before scoring his first single, and in general his innings
'was thoroughly characteristic of his reputation'. He had made 38 in
just over an hour and a half, and the score was 86 for 1, when he fell
to 'the best ball of the day', one from Noble that 'pitched on the off
and knocked the leg stump out of the ground, being at the same
time of such perfect length that the batsman was completely beaten'.
His 38 turned out to be top score of an innings that folded badly to a
total of 145. Australia then made 289, leaving England with a target
of 339 and about an hour's batting on the second evening. Abel
opened with Jessop, but the next day the *Sheffield Daily Telegraph*
asked 'whether it was wise to put Abel in first last night, after so
hard a knock as he had received on his wrist in the last over of the
Colonial innings'. He made 8 out of 14 before, 'playing back to a
quickly turning ball of Noble's', he was out amid some acrimony:
'Hill at slip fell full length on the ground and secured the ball as it
glanced off Abel's bat. The Surrey man was not quite satisfied, and
appealed to the umpire before leaving. Phillips, however, adjudged
it a fair catch.' On the third day England succumbed by 143 runs
and Australia went one up in the series.

The legendary Fourth Test, at Old Trafford, proved to be Abel's
last. Of the batsmen he and Ranji were subsequently replaced by
Jessop and Hayward, in his case primarily because his fielding was
reckoned to be no longer sharp enough for Test cricket. The details
of the match are all too familiar, but it is easy to forget that masked
by the major tragedy of poor Fred Tate was another drama in its
way just as piquant. In the first innings Abel had made 8 when, on a
drying wicket, he 'played forward to Saunders, and the ball travelled
off the shoulder of his bat to Armstrong in the slips'. But it was not
until the final afternoon that Abel really came centre stage, when,
soon after lunch, he joined Ranji with the score on 72 for 3 and
England needing only 52 more to win. He quickly made four runs,
including giving a hard chance to mid-on, before, with the score on
76, 'a sharp shower drove the cricketers to the pavilion for a quarter
of an hour'. At which point, with England unable to afford a draw,
MacLaren as captain acted decisively. 'The weather looked very

threatening and it was clear, on cricket being again proceeded
with, that Abel had received strict injunctions to hit. He played a
game quite foreign to his ordinary methods, and for a time got on
very well.' Indeed he did, twice driving Trumble to the long-on
boundary, with bold strokes that were in marked contrast to the
seeming inability of Ranji at the other end to lay bat on ball. Cardus
in his marvellous account, 'By Three Runs', caught the intensely
fluctuating mood:

> Thousands of eyes turned away from Ranji and looked to
> Abel for succour. Ah, this is better – the pertness of little Abel
> brightened the soul. He made gallant runs – a boundary over
> Hill's head. 'Cheeky' work this – batsmanship with *gaminerie*.
> 'Bravo, Bobby!' shouted the Old Trafford crowd.

On 92 Ranji was leg-before for a duck and Abel 'saluted Jackson
by welting Saunders to square leg for four in the most vigorous
style'. But after adding another single he was bowled by Trumble
as he drove across a break-back: the score was 97 for 5 and, in
twenty-five minutes, he had scored 21 out of 25 by what the
Sporting Life described as 'as good a piece of batting as any in the
day'. The final five wickets could only muster another 23. *The Times*
gave its judgement on the failure:

> Darling seemed to upset the whole English side by the placing
> of his field. He got his men close in, even for such forcing
> players as Jackson and MacLaren. The Englishmen seemed to
> become afraid. Instead of going forward and hitting the bowlers
> off their pitch, they played back cautiously at everything.

On the basis of the various match reports, it does appear that
Abel was an honourable exception to this charge of timidity. Acting
on his captain's orders, and breaking the batting habits of a lifetime,
he had come within an ace of pulling it off for England, a triumph
that would have crowned his career. Of such, he no doubt did not
reflect in the players' room afterwards as Braund with his handker-
chief tried to comfort the distraught Tate, is the difference between
being a planet and a star.

Chapter Four

THE BATSMAN

And then there is Robert Abel, one of the curiosities of the cricket
field. Abel brought no natural advantages to the art or practice of
batting. Indeed, the contrary was the case. He was short in stature
and not possessed of strong physique. You cannot say that he exactly
had a theory of batting. You do not try to teach a boy to bat like Abel
as you teach him to bat like Hayward. Robert Abel was an unconscious
artist, and he still remains an enigma. The most careful analysis of
cricket and cricket methods has not yet explained to us how and why
Abel succeeded. He was the 'little wonder' of his time; and we still
wonder at our recollections of him.

CONTEMPORARIES SHARED THE sense of wonder expressed by the
cricket journalist Colonel Philip Trevor, writing here in 1921. How
did he do it? Certainly, unlike the celebrated Hampshire batsman
of the 1890s, not by Pooreing over textbooks. According to Pridham,
Abel was 'not of a studious nature' and claimed 'that he had never
read a book on cricket in his life'. While as for composing treatises
on the subject, he presumably took rather the same line as Ranji,
that 'a man who is engaged in heavy brain-work, such as writing a
book on cricket, cannot expect to be at his best in the cricket field'.
It is true that in 1894 there appeared a book under Abel's name
called *Cricket and How to Play It*, but this turned out (though without
acknowledging the fact) to be a word-for-word reprint of John
Wisden's treatise of the same title published in 1862. The following
year, in a revised edition, certain amendments were made, prompting the *Cricket Field* to remark, with justifiable sarcasm, on how 'one
misses the touching allusions to such ancient worthies as Willsher
and Jackson, with whose play Abel must have made acquaintance
at a very early age indeed'. But the amendments were in fact
minimal and the sense of anachronism, let alone plagiarism, still
absurd. Nor was Abel's contribution very much greater to a book
edited in 1903 by E. F. Benson and Eustace H. Miles, with the
alluring title *The Cricket of Abel, Hirst, and Shrewsbury*. The book
was merely a general cricket manual, and all that these three
latter-day worthies did was to pose for some photographs and

apparently pass on the odd apophthegm to the compilers. ' "Play
with the feet," says Abel to all who have feet to play with.' And
about forward play: 'Over one's bat comes one's head: as Abel says,
one must get above the ball and smell it.'

Much more revealing about Abel's conscious, underlying
approach was a piece entitled 'Some Hints on Batting' that he
contributed to P. C. Standing's 1902 anthology *Cricket of Today and
Yesterday*. The piece may have been retouched, but it still reads as
authentically Abel's, above all the pragmatic, semi-autobiographical
opening sentences:

> Though a great deal has been said about style in batting, and
> coaches of the old school insisted upon drilling boys into one
> fixed style on the ground that all other styles were incorrect,
> the best style is the one that comes natural to the batsman.
> After all, the object of batting is to stay in and get runs whether
> you get them in a way that pleases or displeases the stylists.
> You bat well provided you have made them safely. When I
> remember my own early difficulties – and I was at first a very
> nervous batsman with no style at all but with many ideas as to
> how runs should be made – I am forced to say that unless a
> cricketer has a sincere love for the game, is as keen as mustard
> and prepared to study and rectify defects in his methods, he
> will never become a great or even a good bat.

In particular, apart from attitude of mind and constant practice,
Abel regarded two points as cardinal. The first was to adopt a
comfortable-feeling stance: 'Quickness on your feet only comes
when a natural position is taken up, and is essential to good batting.
Indeed, I attribute whatever success I may have achieved to
quickness on my feet.' And secondly: 'Another secret of success is
restraint at the start of your innings. Runs always come easier after
the first 20. The reason is, that you get the pace of the ground, and
know what the ball is doing.' Abel's whole approach was manifestly,
and unashamedly, that of the percentage player. A final passage
from this piece gets one a long way to understanding why he was
indeed 'all there' and such a tough nut to crack:

> Every batsman, even the very greatest, has his limitations,
> and the main object of every aspirant to batting honours

should be to eliminate from his game all strokes that he finds unsuitable to his natural powers, and which he cannot master even by the most diligent study and practice. On the other hand, such strokes as come natural should be diligently cultivated until perfection, and above all accuracy, is attained.

Various quite detailed descriptions of Abel's style exist in the formal literature of the game. Shuter, in his introduction to Abel's reminiscences, had this to say of his old opening partner:

It was not his custom to attempt big hits – indeed in a long day's innings I often used to remark that he had hardly lifted the ball from the ground. He was equally good all round the wicket, being particularly clever on the leg side, and his cutting clean and sure – but his off-driving was especially good, being done with little effort and always well 'along the carpet'.

While from a wicket-keeper's point of view, Lilley remembered Abel as 'a wonderful wrist player' who 'made the old-fashioned cut to perfection'. And later in his book, giving advice on how to late-cut, Lilley noted that 'Mr MacLaren follows the ball, as it were, and places it, whereas Abel used to make a clean hit at it.' It was, however, his on-side play that *Wisden* particularly stressed in its obituary of Abel: 'Very few batsmen have excelled him in scoring in front of short leg, with brilliant and safe forcing strokes off his legs.' Or, in Sir Home Gordon's words, writing at about the same time about the 'sandy-haired tiny little man, frightfully difficult to dislodge', he 'played balls off his legs exceptionally well and made pots of runs by a jab in front of short leg'. Again, though, it is to Fry that one has to look for the full set-piece, namely a marvellously specific commentary on Abel contained in his 1899 compilation *The Book of Cricket*:

He has a curious manner of standing at the wicket (wrapping, as it were, his left leg round the front of his right); he holds his bat close to his thigh, and faces the bowler with all his body above his waist. He scores a great many runs by cutting, being especially skilful at strong strokes off slow bowling behind third man. He has a good stroke, half-cut, half-drive, with which he forces a short ball just in front of point. He plays

forward fairly hard past mid-off and extra-cover. Straight balls
that suit him he drives along the ground past the bowler,
moving out half a step and generally placing the ball slightly
towards the on side. He occasionally hits in the air over mid-
on's head. He is clever at placing the ball away in front of short
leg. His defence is very strong. In playing back he balances
himself skilfully on his right leg and keeps the ball well down.
He has made a study of playing forward for defensive purposes,
so as to smother the ball. His patience is no less wonderful than
his stamina. He rarely attempts a risky stroke, and can gather
a century or two without turning a hair.

Fry's clear admiration for Abel remained undimmed, for as he
wrote in 1945 in the souvenir volume to mark Surrey's centenary:
'Bobby was an accomplished all-round stroke player with a lovely
off-drive and a natural late cut. Very interesting it was to field out to
him. He seemed such a resourceful craftsman.'

The sporting papers and periodicals of Abel's time are of course
littered with descriptions of his batting style. There are far too
many to be quoted exhaustively, and none is as systematic as Fry's
analysis, but a selection from them does give some idea of his
methods at the crease. 'Abel's play on the on side was very good
indeed and brought out frequent applause,' wrote the *South London
Journal* in 1884 in its report of the Surrey versus Australians match.
The next year the *Sportsman* noted how Abel 'never failed to punish
anything pitched up by Ulyett' in the home match with Yorkshire.
In January 1888 the Hobart-based *Mercury* had its first glimpse of
the Guv'nor and, after recording that in the match at Launceston he
'gave the slips and the legs plenty of work', went on: 'He seems
rather fond of getting back to his sticks to play some balls, but is
very cautious, though he plays boldly when a chance offers.' Later
that year the *Empire* attempted a profile of him as a batsman:

He excels Bannerman as a stone wall; but his defence has
nothing stiff about it. Abel lifts his bat shoulder high as the ball
is delivered, and makes a sweep in the air before he brings it
down. For his size he has a good reach; but he is stronger in
playing back than in forward play. He is adept at placing. The
field is brought in, and strengthened in the slips, when he is set.

No journalist could have been more enthusing than 'Felix' (T. P. Horan), writing in the *Australasian* in 1892 at the end of Lord Sheffield's tour: 'To my mind Abel is the sweetest bat in the team. Beautifully free and finished, he makes his strokes in perfect fashion all round the wicket, and his cutting alone is enough to make one's mouth water to copy.' 'Rover' of the *Morning Leader* also had an especially soft spot for Abel, epitomized by his report of that stirring 94 against the Gentlemen in 1896:

It was amazing to watch him get Ernest Smith and Sammy Woods to leg, sometimes from balls that rose as high as his shoulder. Abel seems to be cultivating this beautiful leg-stroke of his. It is not a pull nor a hook so much as a glance, a gentle deflection of a ball that possesses a bias towards the leg side. Such a stroke requires the most perfect timing and the most delicate manipulation of the bat.

Less ecstatic was the *Sporting Life* a few weeks later about his 91 against Kent, observing that 'Abel's play was rather noticeable for skilful placing than any particular brilliancy.' The following year, reporting the home match with Middlesex, the *Daily Mail* had a nice description of Abel as sheet-anchor: 'An occasional cut, an occasional leg-hit, but rarely a drive, came from his bat; but the main thing was that he stayed at the wicket while others came and went.' In 1898, when he made his coveted century against Yorkshire, the *Sporting Life* referred to how 'his powerful play on the leg side and fine off-drives were exquisitely good'. And reporting the same fixture two years later, *The Times* described how, 'in their very different sytles', he and Brockwell put on 85 for the first wicket: 'Brockwell's driving was very good, while Abel, as ever, executed his variety of strokes, and was particularly effective in taking the ball off his leg stump.' The following season the Philadelphian spectator quoted in *Cricket* had nothing to say about Abel's actual batting, but did note that 'while waiting for the ball he delivers a series of quick little taps with his bat in the block'. In 1902 Jephson contributed a column in the *Westminster Gazette* and, describing Abel's innings at Leyton, he wrote: 'In making 150 he never made a bad stroke, gave no chance, cut and drove at his very best, and forced the almost good-length ball off the middle and leg between square leg and mid-on with wonderful precision. I don't think he missed even one.' Finally, in 1904, there was 'Vigornia' of the *Athletic News* writing appreciatively of his 87 at Worcester: 'It was very grateful to see the veteran, Abel, playing with the confidence of old, making forceful strokes on the on side and placing to the off with accustomed accuracy.'

It is a measure of the narrative density of the match reports of that era that at least 3,000 of Abel's runs were specifically described, in terms of either the stroke played or where the ball went. More research in newspaper libraries would produce more annotated runs, but here the tally is 3,180, just under one-tenth of Abel's career aggregate. The terminology employed in these reports is not always as precise as it might be, and cricketing usage anyway is never static, but some sort of statistical picture does emerge. Of these 3,180 runs, Abel definitely or probably scored 1,486 on the on side, with the following break-down: 69 from snicks, 22 from strokes specifically called leg-glances, 15 to long leg, 208 to square leg, 693 to leg, 194 to the on, 25 with pulls, and 260 with on-drives. The total for the off side is 1,300 runs, derived from 96 through or over the slips, 78 with late cuts, 699 with cuts in general, 83 to the off, and 344 with off-drives. The terms present their problems, but if one takes 'leg' to mean rather squarer of the wicket than 'on', then Abel's tendency to play the ball square on either side is fairly unambiguously illustrated. There is no doubt that he could cut exceedingly hard: in 1892, in the Gentlemen versus Players match at the Oval, W. W. Read at point was badly winded by one such stroke, causing play to he held up for three minutes.

394 of these runs are more difficult to allocate to either side of the wicket. 112 of them were scored 'square'. Now the term would invariably mean the off side, but in the late nineteenth century its purpose seems, as far as one can tell, to have been dual. The other 282 came from unspecified drives – with perhaps the majority (on the basis of Fry's observation) going to the on. It was in fact an on-drive that brought Abel his seven against Middlesex in 1894, which was the most runs off a single stroke at the Oval since the introduction there of boundary rails, ending the custom of every-thing having to be run out. Reports differed as to whether the bowler was Rawlin or Stoddart, but *Cricket*'s columnist did offer a certain gloss on the episode, which occurred soon after Abel had reached his century:

The match was played wide on the Clayton Street side, and the ball went close to the boundary in the direction of the Vauxhall Gate. On its return Phillips fumbled the ball in forwarding it to the wicket, but in any case six had been made before it reached him. The extension of the banks and retirement of the football pavilion has made the ring at the Surrey ground, I should think, the widest in any county enclosure, or very near it.

Indeed, as he came into his prime, drives became more and more a feature of Abel's batting: whereas up to 1893 they brought him only twenty-one per cent of his runs, in the years from 1894 they earned him just over a third. Wickets were getting ever better, his self-confidence was increasing, and in consequence the field no doubt did not come in quite as it once had done when he was batting. No mid-on or mid-off, though, ever confused him with Jessop or MacLaren.

To put Abel's round-the-wicket batting figures into some perspective, it is important to realize that most of his runs were scored during the heyday of off-theory bowling, one of the more negative phases in bowling history. It is obvious, then, that to have scored so many runs on the on side he must have played there a lot of balls that were not going down the leg. But by around the turn of the century a general shift in direction was starting to occur. In Standing's 1902 miscellany, Rhodes noted how since the start of his career he had seen 'the ball breaking from the off almost entirely change in favour of the leg-break theory'. But if that is when it started to end, when exactly off-theory proper came in, with its medium-paced practitioners bowling outside the off stump to packed off-side fields, is a matter of some debate. Perhaps it was shortly before Abel's time, to judge by a remark in the 1890 *Wisden* about 'those somewhat degenerate days in the latter half of the 1870s, when the majority of English professionals thought that the whole art of bowling consisted in pitching wide of the off stump for catches'. To which one must add that other sources indicate that this 'degenerate' practice was by no means extinct by 1890.

A prime target of the theory was Shrewsbury, around whom the marked revival of professional batting in the 1880s was centred and who up to his death in 1903 remained, in the eyes of most critics, the leading professional batsman of the day. The theory did not much help to get him out – he was, everyone agreed, a batsman of almost inexhaustible patience – but it did slow him down, to an extent that declining attendances at Trent Bridge were often attributed to his sluggish rate of scoring. He was a severely correct batsman, at his best playing from his back foot on difficult wickets, and, as Lyttelton observed in 1899, 'unable at any time of a long innings to force the pace, he scores at the same rate when he has got 200 runs as when he has got 10'. Shrewsbury was also intimately associated with the controversial art of pad play, about which *The Jubilee Book* had some interesting words:

> The skill with which he uses his legs on treacherous wickets is nothing short of miraculous. His comrade in arms, William Gunn, can also play this game very ably; so too can Mr Stoddart and Mr Jackson – a fact not generally known. The difference between the play of the two professionals and the two amateurs is, that the former make use of the method when it is not necessary to resort to it, whereas Mr Stoddart and Mr Jackson only do so when there is no other course open save wild slogging.

It is a suggestive passage, not least the phrase 'a fact not generally known'. If the 1880s saw a renaissance of professional batting, the 1890s were characterized by an equally impressive counter-renaissance of amateur batting, headed by Stoddart, Jackson, Jessop, Fry, Ranji and MacLaren, belatedly taking some of the annual burden off the Old Man's shoulders. Inevitably there was a tendency to compare the more cautious methods of the professional batsmen unfavourably with those of the relatively carefree amateurs, for whom style could be as important as mere occupation of the wicket. It is possible to exaggerate this contrast in basic approach, but the famous description by Cardus of MacLaren's graceful, gallery-pleasing, above all ineffably noble quack is not easily forgotten. And Abel, whose double centuries were as profoundly unclassical as his noughts, suffered more than most by the comparison.

Some of the major strengths and weaknesses of Abel as a batsman were delightfully commemorated for contemporary readers in the

best-selling *The Jubilee Book of Cricket* (1897) that Fry in effect
co-authored with Ranji. In it at one point they go through, from a
bowler's point of view, an innings by an imaginary side, in fact
Surrey. Cain and Stockwell open the batting, with Cain receiving
first ball. 'He takes block. "Does it cover 'em both, Tom? Thank
you." He looks round to see where the fieldsmen are placed, finds
them in normal positions, settles himself, and indicates by his
manner that he is ready.' The first four balls from the right-arm fast
bowler are all good-length on the off stump and to them 'Cain plays
carefully forward without scoring'. The final ball of the over, an
attempted yorker that is a full toss, 'is forced gently but firmly past
the bowler' for a single. At the other end a medium-pace left-armer
bowls his first two on a good length outside the off stump: 'Cain
shapes twice for a cut, but lets both pass without making a stroke.'
He then 'snicks the third ball off his leg stump for three'. So it goes:

> Cain is a slow, patient, steady bat, with not the remotest
> intention of risking his wicket. Nothing can tempt him to have
> a go. But he is apt to lunge out at good-length balls rather
> prematurely, has a weak half-hearted stroke between the
> slips, and does not find a fast, short, quick-rising ball much to
> his taste. He is inclined to retire slightly towards short-leg, and
> 'spar' at fast, straight balls.

The medium-pacer tries in vain to get him to have a go, presenting
him with a couple of half-volleys, but 'Cain has played them, if
possible, more carefully than the good-length balls'. The other batsmen, however, have been less restrained: Stockwell, Netherland,
and Strawyard are all out, bringing in at number five H. H. Rush,
who at once starts hitting freely. 'All this time Cain has been
playing as steadily as ever. He has been badly missed once by
short-slip, and since then has shaped much better. Without forcing
the game he is scoring consistently on both sides of the wicket.'
Finally the fast bowler returns, with Cain apparently on his way to a
century:

> He has to take the fast bowler's first over, and plays it as
> carefully as ever. The last ball of the over – a very fast one, as
> the bowler meant it to be – bumps unexpectedly. Cain flinches

ever so slightly, just touches the ball, and is caught by short-slip. He cocks his eye thoughtfully at the spot where the ball pitched, walks out and pats the slight roughness there for the benefit of his successor, and then waddles off to the pavilion amid cheers. He acknowledges his reception by lifting his faded chocolate cap in a way entirely peculiar to himself.

Was Abel in fact really so vulnerable to the slip trap? Out of the 504 times that he was out caught (from a total of 921 dismissals), details of where he was caught can be ascertained for 440 of them. The breakdown is instructive. Two hundred and sixty-five of these 440 catches were definitely taken on the off side: 122 at slip or cover-slip (i.e. second slip), 55 at point (then rather nearer to the wicket than now), 38 at mid-off or extra mid-off, 26 at cover point or extra cover-point, 21 at third man, and one each at silly point, deep point, and deep mid-off. By contrast, he was definitely caught on the on side only 49 times, despite scoring more than half his runs there. He was out 21 times at mid-on, 15 times at short leg, sharp short leg, forward short leg, or short square leg, seven times at short mid-on, three times at deep square leg, twice at square leg, and once at long-on. The preponderance of off-side dismissals is accentuated by the fact that he was also caught 63 times by the wicket-keeper and 62 times by the bowler, presumably in both positions much more often to the off than the on. Finally, he was caught once 'in the long field', but wherabouts exactly is not stated. So, if one reckons that 'the box' (to use the phrase of the time) extended from wicket-keeper through slip and cover-slip until it reached point, then he was caught in that Bermuda Triangle of batsmanship some 241 out of 440 times. Even the *Morning Leader* could not avoid a certain weariness of tone when it described his dismissal off Hearne at Catford Bridge in 1896: 'Abel was out as he is nine times out of ten when he makes a little score. He just poked out his bat and the slipper did the rest. It was a good catch, but it was a villainous stroke.' Not that he was by any means always caught there or thereabouts merely poking. In 1901, for instance, he was caught cutting at least four times, falling twice to point and twice to third man (including the debatable catch at Canterbury). And the following year, on the only occasion he was out to Trumper, he hit across a long hop and was caught at slip.

the first Surrey wicket

bowled Humphreys.

caught Brann

Sussex *v* Surrey at Hove, 1892. Abel c Brann b Humphreys 61

Certainly, though, there was not much point expecting a catch if you fielded in the deep to Abel. It is a mark of Grace's cunning that he thrice induced him to hole out to deep square leg: in 1886 when Abel's was the last wicket to fall for the Players at Lord's; two years later at Clifton (assuming that it was deep); and in the Gentlemen versus Players match of 1897 at the Oval, after Abel had made only 30. 'That such an astute and sound batsman should have fallen into Grace's ancient trap was certainly surprising,' was the *Sporting Life*'s understandable comment on that final leg of the three-card trick. Otherwise, catches in the deep off Abel's bat were few and far between: in 1889, after he had batted the South to a safe position at Old Trafford, he was caught at deep mid-off; in 1897, as Surrey went for quick runs on an impossible wicket at Leicester, he gave his catch to the long field; the following year, on a sticky at Bradford, he was caught at deep point by Jackson off Rhodes for 6; and in 1899 his innings of 167 against Hampshire, characterized by unusually powerful driving, ended with a hit to long-on. Not many rushes of blood, in other words, in virtually a quarter of a century of batting.

It is a remarkable fact that during that lengthy span Abel was out leg before wicket even less often than he was caught in the deep. Shacklock (then of Derbyshire) was the first bowler to dismiss him thus, in 1885, followed the next year by Thornton of Kent, who got Abel to 'put his leg in front of a lob'. In 1888 Ferris did him twice, first at Melbourne and then at the Oval. There followed a gap of eleven years, before Trott for Middlesex got the nod at Lord's. And finally, of course, there was that bathetic LBW that Somerset's Robson procured at Taunton in 1904. By comparison, Abel was stumped as many as thirty-one times in his career. Although it was his wife who effectively got him out at Hove in 1891, what happened more often than not was that, batting on a bad wicket and trying to get to the pitch of the ball, he gave a fairly easy stumping. On a few occasions, though, especially against the western spinners Tyler and Townsend, he overreached himself and found the bails being smartly taken off. Interestingly, he was stumped only thirteen times up to the end of 1893, but eighteen times afterwards, a further indication of his increasing willingness to drive. Thirty-one was also the number of times that Abel was run out. Most of these dismissals are attributed in the match reports to mutual misunderstanding between the partners, but on at least ten occasions the run out does definitely seem to have been Abel's fault, whereas his partner is specifically blamed only three times. These run outs occurred at a fairly steady rate in the course of his career, with three the most that he ever chalked up in a single season, in 1892 and 1899. He was also at odd times palpably responsible for running out his partner (one thinks of Brockwell at Taunton in 1897), but not so often that he was ever reckoned to be a poor judge of a run: that his last appearance at Trent Bridge should have been marked by his being run out going for an impossible third was another of the ironies of the 1904 season. Finally, in the oddities department, there were the two times he was out hit wicket. In 1887, versus Lancashire at the Oval, in playing a ball from Briggs he 'let the bat slip out of his grasp and hit the wicket'; while two years and various catapulting expeditions later, Briggs again had him out in this rather ignominious way, though this time he was playing for Pilling's Eleven and Abel for Hall's Eleven in a low-scoring end-of-season match at Holbeck, Leeds. There would have been worse times to be out hit wicket.

Abel also was bowled 347 times, but match reports shed light on less than a quarter of these dismissals. One can still, however, glean some quite revealing information. Forty-eight times it is mentioned which stump was hit: twenty-two times it was the leg stump, sixteen the middle, eight the off, and once the middle and off; while at Taunton in 1901 he was out when a ball from Cranfield 'grazed the off stump and, curiously enough, shook off the leg bail'. What sort of ball was it that tended to bowl him, often leg stump? From the sketchy details available, one can say that at least fourteen times it was a ball breaking back on Abel, compared with at least six times a ball going away from him; while seven times the ball was described as a yorker or a shooter, compared with fourteen times being a 'trimmer' or a 'bailer', a discrepancy one would expect from a small batsman. In terms of what Abel was trying to do to counter these balls, he is reported as thirteen times playing forward, to eight times playing back; while on as many as fifteen occasions he was trying to play the ball to leg. Ten times he was bowled off either his pads or his body; and he played-on no less than forty-nine times, most painfully in 1893 against Guttridge (then of Sussex), when he 'played a ball hard on to his foot, and thence into his wicket'. What can one conclude from all this inevitably rather bitty information? Perhaps not all that much, except to say that the 'typical' ball that bowled Abel was the one coming in to him that he tried to work to leg, got an inside edge to, and hit leg stump. If indeed he played with a bat that was not always perfectly straight, it sounds a plausible enough type of dismissal. On the other hand, he scored such 'pots of runs' in the mid-wicket area that clearly one is considering here (as with all his types of dismissal) a relative rather than an absolute weakness.

These grainy questions of technique have a certain perennial fascination, quite distinct from aggregates and averages. Fry later recalled how in 1904, planning the first number of his own magazine, he had visited J. M. Barrie:

He spent the best part of an hour extracting from me in detail how the more prominent players of the day made their runs

or got their wickets. Especially he wanted to know whether
Bobby Abel really did play with a cross-bat and whether I
thought that Lockwood threw. I said 'No' to both these libels.

Fry took the same line in an article called 'Now and Then' that he
wrote in the *Cricketer* in 1945:

It is a fact that the old conventions were sometimes pushed to
absurdity. For instance, Bobby Abel, when he was one of the
three or four most successful and accomplished of our batsmen,
was several times left out of representative teams because a
legend budded into circulation in high places that 'he did not
play forward with a straight bat'. I fielded out while he scored
several centuries and never saw him play crooked; but the
idea among eminent purists that he was a heretic against the
quasi-religious dogma was enough to condemn him – ridiculous
in the case of such a run-maker, but true.

Few others, though, shared Fry's memory of a straight bat.
Sewell stated bluntly that Abel 'never had one', and Hodgson
recalled how 'it was palpable that his bat was frequently out of the
perpendicular'. Even Trevor sat on the fence:

It was always said he held his bat crooked. Did he, I wonder?
Was it crooked at the exact moment he put it to the ball?
Instantaneous photography had not reached its present
perfection when Abel was in his zenith, or it might have
enlightened us in regard to that matter.

While as for the grand inquisitors of Abel's time, they had, as Fry
said, no doubts at all:

So many runs are scored by batsmen who are not really sound
first-rate batsmen. In one of the largest scorers of the day –
namely, Abel – we see a batsman who generally plays with a
crooked bat. He has great merits, he has much patience, a
wonderfully good eye, and is a splendid judge of length; but it
is a fair assumption that run-getting on the modern wickets is
far too easy if so many runs can be scored by a batsman who
plays so crooked.

A rare portrait of a clean-shaven Abel: 1885   (*MCC*)

Agreement made this day of October One thousand eight hundred and eighty eight **Between** Robert Gardner Warton Mayor, R.P. of the one part and R. Abel of Surrey professional Cricketer of the other part

And first the said R. Abel agrees with the said Robert Gardner Warton as a professional cricketer to accompany him on a cricketing tour to South Africa for a period (inclusive of the duration of passage there and back) of about four months from the twenty second November One thousand eight hundred and eighty eight and to play in all such cricket matches as the said Robert Gardner Warton may require.

In consideration whereof the said Robert Gardner Warton Agrees with the said R. Abel to pay to him the sum of One hundred pounds as follows Such a sum as he may require not exceeding Thirty pounds prior to embarcation for Cape Town A further sum of Forty pounds and the balance if any of the said sum of Thirty pounds between the time of disembarcation at Cape Town and the embarcation on return passage to England and the balance of such One hundred pounds during the homeward voyage.

The said Robert Gardner Warton further agrees to pay reasonable travelling and boarding expenses of the said R. Abel during the tour.

Witness,

R Gardner Warton Maj:

Sign here Robert Abel
Oct 88

Abel's contract to tour the Cape in 1888–89   (*MCC*)

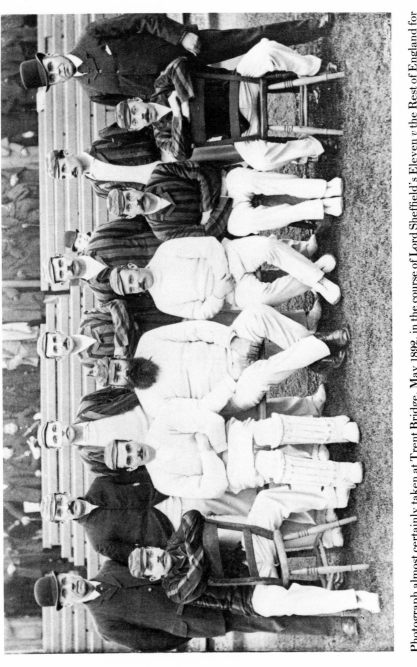

Photograph almost certainly taken at Trent Bridge, May 1892, in the course of Lord Sheffield's Eleven *v* the Rest of England for Alfred Shaw's benefit. *Standing:* Carpenter, Attewell, Lohmann, Read, M., Bean, Sharpe, Thoms. *Seated:* Briggs, G. MacGregor, W. G. Grace, Peel, A. E. Stoddart, Abel (*MCC*)

Photograph by E. HAWKINS & CO. *Your obedient Servant* 32, 33 & 38, Preston Street, Brighton

Robt Abel

Abel in 1895

The Oval, from Alcock's *Famous Cricketers and Cricket Grounds* (1895)

Sam Apted, ground-keeper at the Oval (1896)   (*MCC*)

Surrey in 1898. *Standing:* Lockwood, Lees, Brockwell, Mr V. F. S. Crawford, Wood. *Seated:* Holland, Mr D. L. A. Jephson, Mr K. J. Key (Captain), Richardson, Hayward. *Front:* Baldwin, Abel

(*The British Library*)

The Surrey professionals taking the field, *v* Middlesex at the Oval in 1898. Abel, almost certainly on the left, has the gait of someone who has done this before   (*MCC*)

Abel acknowledging the applause after his innings of 357 not out *v* Somerset in 1899. But since Abel carried his bat, why are the Somerset fielders apparently waiting around for the next batsman? There seems no obvious explanation
(*MCC*)

Shaping for a square cut   (*MCC*)

'Well kept down!'   (*MCC*)

A contemporary cartoon (1899)

(*Above*) Surrey *v* Lancashire at the Oval, 1900. Richardson is bowling

(*Below*) Gentlemen *v* Players at the Oval, 1901. Abel playing R. E. Mo▸

...ard; Abel is almost certainly at point   (*The British Library*)

...the on; Quaife is at the bowler's end   (*The British Library*)

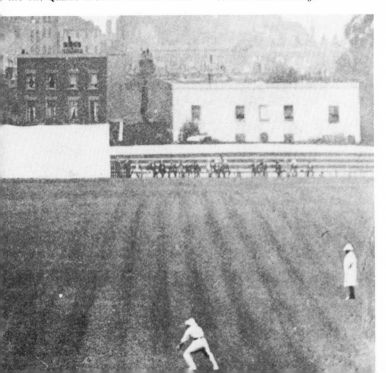

The Third Test *v* Australia at Bramall Lane in 1902. England taking the field at the start of Australia's second innings; Abel is coming out fourth behind MacLaren, Jackson and Fry   (*The British Library*)

Players of England *v* the Australians at the Oval, 1902. Abel plays

The Fourth Test v Australia at Old Trafford in 1902. Abel and Palairet going out
to open England's first innings   (*The British Library*)

e off during his innings of 35. Hayward (74) is the non-striker
(*The British Library*)

A wonderful player, this little man,
   For with *patience* the seed was sown,
He has every stroke in the 'Cricket Book',
The long-handled drive and the short-arm'd h
But he hasn't acquired the 'picture' look,
   'Tis a style that is quite his own.
                  (D. L. A. Jephson, *A Few Overs,*)

Albert Craig, 'The Surrey Poet',
probably towards the end of his life
(*MCC*)

Surrey *v* Worcestershire at the Oval,
May 1904. Abel, in his last season,
going out to open the batting with
Hayward   (*The British Library*)

A portrait of Abel in 1904   (*MCC*)

Thus wrote 'An Old Cambridge Blue' in *The Times* in his review of the 1901 season, an indictment followed up the next year by the same paper's scathing description of Abel's distinctly non-perpendicular attempt to play Jessop in the Gentlemen versus Players match at Lord's. Lyttelton in 1899 gave his explanation for the great heresy:

He moves his right foot to certain balls, such as good-length balls on the leg stump to which he plays back, and consequently often plays with a crooked bat. Jupp [Surrey's diminutive stonewall opener of the 1860s and 1870s, in many ways Abel's spiritual ancestor] in old days had the marvellous knack of almost running away from fast, shortish bowling on the leg stump, and leaving a more or less horizontal bat in front of the wicket, the extraordinary part of the performance, however, consisting in the fact that Jupp used somehow to stop the ball. Abel does not move his foot so far as Jupp did, but he often plays crookedly.

Lyttelton then clinched his case by citing the Lord's Test of 1896:

Jones was bowling, and the ball got up a little, but Abel had shifted his right foot, and his bat was not straight, neither was his left shoulder forward, and the ball, after striking the bat, was bound to go up. This it did, and had Eady held the easy chance the result of the match might have been different.

Certainly there was an ingrained habit at work, for as Bettes-worth, a whole-hearted admirer, noted in 1904: 'Abel does not play with a straight bat, and he shifts his feet to suit each ball, while often he draws right away from the wicket, even to a slow bowler, as if he were afraid of the ball.' Yet according to the *Jubilee Book*, both these Surrey openers tried hard to overcome the horizontal tendency:

The great Harry Jupp is said to have practised daily in front of a looking-glass in order to make sure of playing with a straight bat. He had a chalk line on the floor, and used to swing his bat up and down it. They tell me Bobby Abel does this too

nowadays; and yet they say he does not play with a straight
bat. At any rate, such practice shows a proper feeling about
the game.

And perhaps, in fact, though one will never know, Abel's bat was
a bit straighter for more of the time than the critics allowed. Such
at least was the view of William Caffyn, the Lohmann of the 1850s,
when he came to write his reminiscences in 1899:

> Abel, that most wonderful of all little players, is still well to the
> fore. The two great secrets of his success have been un-
> doubtedly a straight bat and patience. His defence is as strong
> as a brick wall. It used to be said that he did not play with *quite*
> a straight bat. I once asked a cricketer if this really was the
> case. '*It is quite straight enough!*' I was curtly informed; 'and so
> you'd find out after you'd bowled at him for three or four hours!'

No doubt Barrie also took the point when he received a similar, if
less curt, flea in the ear from Fry.

Closely linked of course to the question of the straight or otherwise
bat and the instinctive movement towards leg was the equally
burning issue of whether or not Abel could play fast bowling.
Various of his performances in big matches at Lord's around the
turn of the century suggest unequivocally that he could not, but
against them must be set his two innings of 94 in 1896 and, also at
Lord's, his 98 in 1900. It is clear that Abel was generally reckoned to
be susceptible to the fast men. Jephson in 1902 cited a leading
cricketer as having recently said to him that 'there had not been a
fast bowler in this country for the last six or seven years who at the
start of an innings of Robert's had not, to use a technical phrase,
done his level best to bump him out'. Did they succeed? Fry as
usual defended the Guv'nor's reputation: 'It is absurd to say that
Abel cannot play fast bowling. The fact that Abel is such a perfect
master of medium-pace bowling does not mean that he cannot make
a good job of the faster stuff.' A few years later, in his 1904 profile,
Bettesworth took a similar line:

> It is true that Abel is commonly supposed to be unhappy when
> opposed to fast bowling, although it is not on record that any

fast bowler has said so. But even on the most dangerous wickets he has often played a great game against the fastest men in the world; now steering the ball through the slips to the boundary, now getting his head out of its way in the nick of time, now taking it almost off his nose and placing it cleverly to leg.

Other former opponents subsequently spoke up for Abel in this respect. Jessop himself, Abel's scourge in 1902, wrote twenty years later:

For a man of his tiny stature it was extraordinary how he succeeded in getting so well over the ball, especially against fast bowling, which he was presumed to have by no means a singular distaste for. At one time anyone possessed of sufficient pace was supposed to be equal to the task of dismissing Bobby in the first few overs. Bobby may have preferred medium and slow bowling to that of the ultra-fast description; for all that, year after year he continued to pile up huge scores against the fastest bowling of the day.

And Lord Hawke concurred:

All through his fine career the remark used to be heard that Bobby Abel was afraid of fast bowling. I have never known many professionals who relished it, because, as their bread-and-butter depends on their playing, they naturally do not want to be knocked about. I have seen the diminutive Bobby coolly playing the fastest bowling, which was ripping up the stumps of his comrades, and never appearing in difficulties.

Such was the formal case for the defence. What one really has to do, though, is to see how Abel got on during his career as a whole when confronted by the major fast bowlers of the day.

It is impossible to be comprehensive, but in England the main bowlers of real pace whom Abel faced over the years were arguably Crossland, Mold, Woods, Jessop, Bradley, Heseltine, and Kortright – the last five of whom were all part of the remarkable phase of amateur fast bowling of the mid-1890s to the turn of the century. Crossland, described by Altham as 'among the professionals the solitary express bowler of real class between Fred Morley and Tom Richardson', had been drummed out of the first-class game by the time that Abel became an established batsman. Before then, though, he twice bowled (or whatever) Abel for a duck in 1882 and might have been expected to do so the following year at the Oval when he took 7 for 34, except that Abel made 10 not out and, according to *Wisden*, 'stood up to the fast bowling in capital style'. In his memoirs Abel recalled how in the course of that innings Crossland had knocked him off his legs three times.

During the 1890s Lancashire's successor to Crossland as their fast bowler with a doubtful action was the formidable Arthur Mold. Abel's record against him was mixed: as tended to be the case with him and fast bowlers, his highs were very high, his lows unusually low. Six times in county matches Mold bowled him for 15 or less, but Abel made 146 in 1890, 148 in 1898, and 178 in 1899. In the second of these centuries, at Old Trafford, 'Mold's bowling flew about very awkwardly' at the start and Abel on 3 was missed at cover-slip, while later in the innings he 'played one ball from Mold on to his wickets without removing the bails', but overall it was a fine defensive display in five and a quarter hours.

Woods was at his fastest during Abel's middle period. He first came to the Oval in 1888 for Cambridge University as, in the words of the *Sportsman*, 'their crack about whom so much has been said', but he was 'severely knocked about' by Abel, who scored 160 out of a total of 312. On subsequent occasions Woods took partial revenge, six times getting him out for the Gentlemen at either Lord's or the Oval for a score of under 50, including in 1892 with 'a very fast ball' that took leg stump. It was a boon for Abel that in the course of his 357 in 1899 Woods was only able to use himself sparingly, though by then he had probably taken his measure.

Two fast bowlers who often operated in tandem for the Gentlemen were Jessop and Bradley. Between 1894 and 1902 Jessop for his various teams eight times bowled Abel for scores of under 25, though of course in the Lord's match of 1900 the batsman emerged on top, even if eventually falling to Jessop in each innings. Abel twice scored centuries when Bradley was in Kent's attack, while at the Oval in 1900 Bradley was with Jessop in the Gentlemen's putative strike-force when Abel 'took tea' (in Jessop's phrase) so commandingly with the bowlers. But in general it was Bradley who held the whip hand, dismissing Abel seven times for under 15, at least twice caught at third man. Fairly typical of this dominance was the match at Blackheath in 1898. Abel was held back at the end of the first day and batted at number six on the following morning. Bradley was immediately brought on, with results told in the rather perky words of the *Star*:

> We had a little spell of little Abel. Bobby opened with a fine two square cut off Alec Hearne, and followed it up with two fours on the leg side off Bradley. But the fast bowler had terrors for Abel, who, after dodging a ball nearly as high as his head, was clean bowled, playing all across a fast ball.

The second innings was not much more convincing, Abel twice being dropped at slip off Bradley before being run out for 32.

But at that particular time Abel would probably have preferred facing Bradley than Hampshire's Christopher Heseltine. In 1897 at Southampton he took strike against Heseltine for a total of three balls: off the first he was nearly caught by Hill in the slips; off the second Hill did catch him; and off the third Quinton caught him at slip. The following year, with this pair on an admittedly 'kicking' wicket behind him, he travelled to meet Heseltine at Portsmouth. Again it was pistols for two and coffee for one, Abel being 'caught at third man in trying to place the first ball, a full pitch, to leg'. In the second innings Surrey needed only 96 to win and secured them for the loss of three wickets: Abel did not bat, presumably preferring to nurse his honour in the pavilion. Later confrontations with Heseltine produced a few reasonable scores, including 93 at Southampton in 1901, but he was not really the same bowler after his return from the Boer War. Abel, meanwhile, had been consolidating his position as at least the second most popular 'Bobs' in the country.

He had also been continuing his long-standing duel with Kortright. It began at Leyton in 1893, before Essex had attained first-class status, with Abel being bowled by him in the first innings for 10, but at least in the second avoiding being one of his five yorked victims, as Kortright again devastated the Surrey batting. This was the season that marked Kortright's coming to fame as the fastest English bowler yet seen, though he was never to play in a Test and did not always turn out regularly for Essex. Two years later Abel made him

toil at the Oval as he scored 217, including reaching his 150 with a
five to leg off him; while in the return match he made 88, out of an
eventual total of 214, before being one of six batsmen clean bowled
by Kortright in the space of fifteen balls. 1896 started similarly:
Kortright at the Oval 'led off at his most terrific pace' and had Abel
on 2 dropped at cover-slip, but Abel then went on to amass 231,
including 15 in an over from the spent terror; at Leyton three
months later, however, Abel had made only 10, standing up to
Kortright 'without flinching', when his 'middle stump became very
flighty at the advance of a Kortright extra special'. The following
year Abel was again at Leyton: early on off Kortright he 'put up a
ball to short leg, but there was no one to reach it', and made 82
before returning a full toss, which Kortright, 'following up some
distance, easily caught'.

Then in 1898 came the real high noon. At Leyton in May, on a
poor wicket, he was caught at cover-slip off Kortright's fourth ball
for a duck; and then in July came the double débâcle, leg stump
each time for 7 and 5, against the Gentlemen at Lord's. 'To see a
man run away as Abel did from Kortright is a painful sight,' Lyttelton
subsequently wrote about the match; and in its immediate aftermath,
the *Sporting Life* flatly stated that 'Abel's dislike to Kortright's
bowling is well known'. The following week Essex visited the Oval,
and Abel responded to the implicit challenge with scores of 148 and
53, according to *The Times* 'playing Kortright with confidence and
scoring freely off him'. Hostilities were more or less suspended in
1899 (Abel had Bradley mostly on his mind), but 1900 saw some
further good scores against Kortright: 68, 4 (bowled), 12 (bowled),
and 137 for Surrey, 30 and 98 for the Players. The century at
Leyton was a rapid and fairly dramatic affair: Kortright 'clean beat'
him before he had scored; and not long afterwards he scored three
fours in an over off him, 'although his third four was extremely
lucky, for getting out of the way of a ball to the leg stump he just
snicked it to leg'. This was perhaps the occasion when, as recalled
by Perrin, the fast bowler blew up:

> It was bad enough when Abel ran away and chopped yorkers
> off the middle stump through the slips; but when he ran away
> so far that he cut him inside the leg stump and to the left of the
> wicket-keeper for four 'Korty' really did say something.

This seems to have been the last of the major confrontations, though in 1901 at Leyton a well-played 71 was followed in the second innings by Kortright getting him caught for 12. Overall, Abel's record against Kortright, whatever his methods, was surely fair enough, if not so stunning as to efface the memory of his performances in W. G.'s birthday match. Perhaps the last word should go to that occasion. Abel apparently, according to Pridham, was being 'chaffed' about his two low scores: to which he replied 'that he had a wife and several small children, and that there were plenty of bowlers, besides Kortright, to make runs off'.

He was no doubt thinking of the run-of-the-mill medium-paced trundlers who, as ever, comprised the backbone of the county bowling. As Fry wrote in his piece on Abel in 1899:

> To total 2,000 runs year after year is a sure sign of something more than mere consistency. It implies a genius for run-getting. Perhaps the reason why Abel achieves such notable figures is that he has acquired in an almost unparalleled degree the art of mastering medium-pace bowling. There is more medium-pace bowling than any other sort of high class in county cricket.

Although he had his early problems against Barlow – several times being out cheaply to him, including twice caught by Hornby – the only bowler in this broad category who really troubled him over the years was the medium-quick Pougher (pronounced 'Puffer') of Leicestershire. Before 1894 most of their meetings were in second-class matches in which Pougher several times dismissed Abel for a small score, though at Leicester in 1887 he fielded out to a century, with a drive for two off his own bowling bringing up the three figures. In that same year he played against Abel at Beckenham for Players of the North versus Players of the South, bowling him for 12; and in 1891, playing for the North at Lord's, he had him caught behind for a duck. In 1894 first-class status was granted and the stakes were raised – a dispensation that Pougher marked by having Abel caught at point for 4 at the Oval and bowled for 6 and 4 on his home ground. The following May he was back at the Oval to play in the Surrey versus England match for W. W. Read's benefit. In the first innings, on a wicket getting plenty of lift, he took 9 for 34,

including Abel with his first ball to him, 'easily caught at slip' by
Ranji. Surrey fared rather better in the second innings, but Abel
only managed to take his match aggregate to 1 before, facing
Pougher, he was out 'playing back and apparently touching the
ball, but losing his wicket'. It was in the context of this match that
Cricket a week or two later cited Abel as having been 'heard to
remark' of Pougher that 'no other bowler bothers him so much'. In
fact, Abel from this point started to master Pougher almost as
efficiently as he did all other bowlers of his pace. Later in 1895 he
made 69 and 38 against him, while in 1896 he was 'particularly
severe' on him in the course of his 152 at home to Leicestershire.
Subsequent encounters likewise saw Pougher coming off distinctly
second best. He had perhaps run out of steam, though on increasingly smooth tracks Abel now took some shunting.

About Abel and slow bowling, Fry expressed much the same
opinion as about Abel and fast bowling: namely, that though not
'shining particularly in dealing with good slow bowling, nevertheless
he plays it well'. While according to the *Cricketer*'s obituary, Abel
was 'quick on his feet to slow bowling'. The equivalent of Pougher
was Somerset's Tyler, a left-armer described by Fry as 'probably
the slowest in pace of all first-class bowlers of this generation',
giving the ball plenty of air and achieving a substantial amount of
finger-spin. Between 1891 and 1896 Tyler got Abel out nine times
for under 50, thrice stumped; while in 1897, in four outings, he
bowled him for 29, 9 ('swiping all across at a breaking ball'), 1 and
30. But again, as with Pougher, Abel then picked up somewhat
after this nadir, scoring four half-centuries against Somerset attacks
including Tyler in the next couple of seasons. It was relevant,
though, that a strain ruled Tyler out of the Oval match in 1899.

Abel also had his difficulties facing the Champion, not only with
the celebrated trap at deep square leg. In the Gentlemen versus
Players match at the Oval in 1896, 'even a past master like the
Guv'nor looked perfectly ridiculous against those slow hanging
deliveries', as 'W. G. bowled to leg with a persistency that must
have been frustrating to Bobby Abel, who made frantic but ineffectual attempts to get him away'. On the whole, though, Abel did
well enough against Grace's bowling and was certainly not his
rabbit. The same applies – despite Humphreys in 1891 and Jephson
in 1900 – to his record against the lobsters: he was altogether too

cautious a batsman to be their regular prey, though it is worth noting, as a curiosity, that at Scarborough in 1892, for the Players, he was caught and bowled off a W. W. Read lob for only 5.

The last few years of his career saw a rising crop of leg-break bowlers, who especially in 1902 presented him with some problems: Braund dismissed him cheaply once for London County and twice for Somerset; Armstrong, in the Australians' first match with Surrey, beat him three times in succession in one over as he played forward; and McGahey at Leyton bowled him twice, for 150 and 0, with, according to Jephson, the variant ball that 'either went quite straight or did an inch or two from the off'. Which brings one to Bosanquet. Abel did not face him all that often after he had left Oxford in 1900 and become a leading leg-break bowler with a new line in twisty-grabs, but when Abel did he was at least twice bested, being caught for 12 in 1902 and bowled for 2 in 1904. It has been said that the first wicket in England that Bosanquet took with his googly was with a ball that bounced four times before it bowled Abel, but the story seems to be apocryphal. Quite apart from the lack of evidence, it sounds unlikely: one feels that Abel would literally have smelt trouble.

An additional question-mark sometimes raised against Abel, though less morally charged than either the crooked bat or the retreat from pace, was that he needed a good wicket on which to bat. Lyttelton had no doubts: 'I cannot but regard Abel as a batsman made first class by the wonderful modern wicket,' he wrote in 1899, arguing that 'nobody who played so crooked could have excelled on the old rough wickets'. The fact, though, that Abel did so much better on the sweet-smelling Oval wickets of the 1890s than almost anywhere else does not in itself prove that he could not bat on wickets affected by rain, a frequent and ubiquitous contingency in those uncovered days (and nights). Abel himself was not insensitive on this score: 'Curiously enough I have been called a hard wicket batsman, but in the summer of 1888 – the wettest one I can recollect – I came out as the finest and most consistent professional batsman in England.' And in 1891 the *Sporting Life*, in its overview of Surrey's year, declared that 'essentially the success of the season was that of Abel, who, despite the many difficult wickets of the past summer, succeeded in scoring more than 900 runs'. It is true that in 1895 'his lack of power to force the game on slow wickets naturally affected him to some extent when the bad weather came', but the following year, again according to *Wisden*, 'while as good as ever on hard grounds he showed a marked increase in judgement and skill when the wickets were affected by rain'. His performance in the deciding match against Australia would alone have almost justified that praise. Two Tests later and he was at perpetually cloud-covered Old Trafford in 1902. For this match he was preferred to Fry, who later wrote: 'This was all right because I had not been making runs. But as it happens I was for value at least 25 per cent a better batsman on a wet wicket than on a dry, whereas Abel was preferably a dry wicket batsman.' Fry's general point may have been valid, but one should add that not only did Abel do well enough in the match in question, but also that his record during the season on wet wickets had hitherto been outstandingly good.

It is not, overall, an issue about which one can come to any very precise conclusions, but one line of statistical inquiry is perhaps worth briefly pursuing. It rests on the assumption that over a period of years totals on bad wickets will tend to be lower than on good ones, often of course dramatically lower. If, then, one compares Abel's contribution to totals under 150 to his contribution to totals of 150 or over, some pointer may in theory emerge. The figures are as follows: batting 232 times in completed totals of under 150, he scored 3,100 out of his side's 24,715 runs, i.e. 12.54%; while batting 585 times in completed totals of 150 plus, he scored 22,871 out of 164,343 runs, i.e. 13.91%. The proportional difference is hardly vast. Or put another way, whereas he was mathematically good for 13 runs in a total of 106, he could be expected to score 39 in a total of 280. Tentatively, then, one may say that Abel was only marginally less of an asset to his side when the wicket was bad. Taking both sets of figures together, incidentally, in an average innings in an average completed total he would make 31 out of 231. But since this never actually happened, it is one of the averages of Abel's life not worth dwelling on overlong.

In 'Some Hints on Batting', Abel offered a couple about coping with a difficult wicket: that 'the secret of success on a drying wicket is to get near to the pitch of the ball to hit or play it'; and that 'on a soft wicket the cut should be avoided', since 'the ball is likely to break back unless the bowler be left-handed and is bowling at the wicket'. Inevitably, though, Abel often found that in practice no amount of 'ikey' little dodges could save him, especially on northern wickets against professional bowlers lethal in helpful conditions. At Trent Bridge in 1889, for instance, he managed only 4 runs as Surrey were bowled out twice on the second day on a 'treacherous ' wicket. The following year at Old Trafford, on a 'very treacherous' wicket, he returned twice to the pavilion on the first day – an experience that he repeated ten years later on the same ground, in the second innings playing on to Sharp 'in trying to protect his face from a rising ball'. Similar fates befell him even at the Oval: in 1891 he was caught at cover-slip for 0 as the Players crashed to 59 all out; five years later he made 3 out of Surrey's first innings total of 45 against Middlesex; and in 1900 he was caught at mid-off by Hirst off Rhodes for 3 again, out of a total of 52 on a drying wicket. It was an era when storm clouds could rage above a batsman's head if he was not out overnight. At the end of the second day in the home match with Gloucestershire in 1892 Surrey were 17 for 0, Abel 13 not out, and still needing 23 more to win. Then came a heavy night storm and the almost inevitable 'very treacherous' wicket the next morning. Surrey won by eight wickets, but 'Abel was in sore difficulties and, after making one or two bad strokes, was completely beaten in the face of a ball from Ferris, and quietly returned it to the bowler'.

Often, confronted by a bad wicket, Abel would decide to gather his rosebuds while he might. At home to Lancashire in 1885, with Surrey needing 116 on a pitch 'wearing very badly' and just making them, he 'played a brilliant innings of 44' and was second out at 55. The *Sportsman* noted how 'by rushing out and meeting most of the balls before they got dangerous, he got on exceedingly well', while according to the *Evening Standard* he had 'seldom hit in better style'. Three years later, in not dissimilar circumstances, he almost pulled it off for the Players on a seemingly impossible wicket at Lord's: with his side needing 78, he scored 30 out of a total of 72, including ten off C. Aubrey Smith's opening over. This policy was never better justified than at Leicester in 1897. After the home team on the first morning had been bowled out for 35, Abel made 19 in twenty minutes before lunch, on the stroke of the interval giving the rare catch to the long field. Surrey then made 164, and before the day was through the opposition had been bowled out again.

At other times, though, Abel preferred to hang in and hope that the wicket would improve and/or his partners would take the offensive. As early as 1883 his patient 37 not out in a total of 122 for 6 helped to steer Surrey home against Derbyshire on a drying wicket after overnight rain. At Old Trafford in 1889 he made a particularly fine 38 in two hours on a 'broken' wicket, being seventh out at 115. 'With the exception of Abel, no one on the side could look at the deliveries of the Lancashire men. The ball played all sorts of pranks, and two or three times Abel narrowly escaped a nasty knock. Too much praise cannot be given him for his fine defensive innings.' And these words of the *Sportsman* were echoed by those of the *Athletic News*, which described how he 'played the splendid balls of Mold and Watson in a style which brought forth the cheers of the crowd'. In 1898, on a difficult Bradford pitch, he even enjoyed an hour of glory (or two and a quarter to be precise) in Yorkshire, making 51 with batting that 'was watchfulness itself'. It is true that Rhodes almost had him caught at point and Haigh 'two or three times narrowly missed disposing' of him, but before he was stumped 'running out to Wainwright' he had 'displayed great skill and judgement'. Temperamentally he was perhaps at his happiest in these long holding operations. One such was on a soft pitch at Edgbaston in 1901, when he 'batted most skilfully for a shade under two hours' and made 34 before he was 'beaten by a very fine ball' from Hargreave, being eighth out. Surrey, however, could only total 109 and lost by 16 runs. The side by then lacked the boldness of a Shuter or a Key to make the most of the meticulous sheet-anchor at the other end.

No one could call Abel a Nat-West batsman. 'McKibbin was obviously bowling for catches, and in one over Abel refused to play at four balls which were wide of the off stump,' reported the *Star* in 1896. Such eschewal perhaps helped to precipitate the decline of off-theory, or at least the more attacking version of the theory, for according to Lyttelton in the 1904 edition of the book he co-edited called *Cricket*: 'A few years ago the prevailing method of bowling was to bowl on the off side for catches, but this is not so common now as formerly because cautious players like Abel got into the habit of leaving the balls together alone.' The upshot was proto-leg-theory, not only on the part of Armstrong. A. C. S. Glover, the Warwicks captain, related in an 1899 interview what he had done in a recent match at the Oval as the runs had inexorably piled up: 'As a last resort I put on Willie Quaife to bowl about six inches off the leg stump, placing nearly all the fielders on the on side. The result was that neither Abel nor Brockwell would touch a ball.' Abel himself was asked once if he ever wished he was a big hitter:

I must own that occasionally I do. At Catford, for instance, I felt that I would give anything to be able to hit. I was in with Baldwin, and we put on six runs in almost an hour. I didn't know what to do, for although the thing was getting almost unbearable, I felt sure that if I began to hit I should get out, and I know that Baldwin felt the same thing about himself.

The chronology is uncertain, but he may have been referring to the low-scoring match in 1893 that was played at the Private Banks' Ground, Catford Bridge. Surrey in the final innings needed 143 to win and lost by 22 runs, but Abel's 44 in three hours was the highest score of the match. At one point he and Baldwin did indeed get bogged down, making in fact 23 runs in an hour, of which Baldwin made six. 'Of course, the Kent bowling required much skill in defence, but it was thought the Surrey professionals should have attempted to quicken the pace of run-getting,' was the comment of *The Times*. Similar criticisms were voiced at steady intervals through the years. 'Under such favourable conditions as regards the pitch and the weather it is not too much to expect that a batsman of his calibre ought to score at a faster rate than 18 runs an hour,' wrote a Sydney paper in 1892 after his 48 against New South Wales in almost three hours. While in 1900, after Abel had batted through the first day against Sussex at the Oval to reach 154 not out, the *Sporting Life* judiciously summed up his performance:

From beginning to end he played a sound, steady game, and batted with all his well-known grace and skill. It was, indeed, a characteristic display. Even at the end of the day, when all the sting had been taken out of the Sussex bowling, and the fieldsmen were apparently weary, he was as cautious as when he first went in.

Was Abel, then, sometimes too cautious for his team's good? According to Lyttelton, he was in the first match against the Australians in 1886:

Surrey had to go in to get 87 runs to win. Abel was playing for an hour and three-quarters, while Garrett and Evans were bowling, every ball dead on the wicket, and during that time laboriously compiled 13 runs. The result of the match was really very doubtful after the fall of the seventh wicket, but Jones, a courageous cricketer, seeing what was the right game, went out and hit Palmer over the ropes for four, and the value of this hit cannot be exaggerated.

A more fateful lack of beef was shown at Cheltenham three years later, arguably costing Surrey the outright championship. He came in at 74 for 3, with Surrey needing 52 more in half an hour. Key hit away freely and the total reached 108 with a few minutes to go, but then Key was out and the match was finally left drawn with Surrey 14 short. Abel finished not out 8 and, according to the *Sportsman*, 'had Key only been backed up by him, the requisite runs would readily have been obtained'. As far as the spectators were concerned, their usual enthusiasm for Abel could naturally wear somewhat thin on his slower days. At Trent Bridge in 1887 'the applause which he received as he walked to the pavilion was equally an acknowledgement of his performance and an expression of relief at his retirement', while at Lord's in 1892 'he was cheered on retiring, but probably on account of his slow play [57 in three and a half hours] not very enthusiastically'. Even the Oval crowd did not suspend all its critical faculties: playing for the South in 1885, Abel 'got Wright away for a trio, the unusual occurrence being greeted with ironical cheers'; and in the course of a stolid Abel-Shrewsbury partnership for the Players in 1898, 'The spectators, dulled by the prevailing somnolence, scarce found interest enough to cheer a stroke for two by the Guv'nor.' Few, though, would have gone so far as the character depicted in one of Sewell's columns in the *Athletic News*:

I shall never forget the story told me by an old Anglo-Indian, possibly with a liver, who was home on leave, and happened to see Abel and Brockwell get that 350 odd for Surrey's first wicket against Hants. Towards the end of the partnership the hat was sent round and duly reached my friend: 'Give anything for the fine stand?' quoth he. 'Tell Mr Abel and Mr Brockwell, if you like, I'll give 'em a sovereign each to get out, sickening – sickening!'

In fact, Abel and Brockwell scored that day at a steady 75 runs an hour, a rate sick-making one would have thought only to the bowlers. As Bettesworth wrote in 1897, the very year of that monster stand: 'It has been urged occasionally – very occasionally – against Abel that he takes a long time in making his runs, but he is by no means a barn door batsman, and few would wish him to alter his style.' And two years later Fry echoed the point: 'He is a very steady and careful player, but is, unless he dislikes the bowling particularly, by no means a slow scorer. He can certainly make very good use of loose or bad length balls.' One of his staunchest defenders on this score was Shuter:

He possessed the reputation of being rather of the 'stonewall' order and there is no doubt that when the necessity arose he could play the role as well if not better than any other living cricketer, but that his character generally as a batsman should come under the above heading I can never admit. I always went to the wicket with the determination to attack the bowlers, nor was I in the habit of wasting much time, but often did I find 'Bobbie' treading closely on my heels in the matter of scoring.

Another Surrey captain, Jephson, writing in 1902, was similarly concerned to vindicate Abel's reputation:

'Oh yes, a very fine player, but terribly slow,' is a remark concerning the little man that we have heard many a time, and not always, I am sorry to say, from men who know nothing of the game. At times I will admit that his methods are open to this criticism, but as a rule he scores very much faster than the generality of spectators and players are prepared to believe.

And Jephson went on to assert that 'Bobby Abel has never to my knowledge played a ball deliberately with his legs, and has let fewer balls pass him on the off side than almost any player I have ever known.' The former theme was confirmed by Trumble who, quoted in the *Athletic News* remarking on the prevalent use by English batsmen in 1899 of pad play outside the off stump, stated that, 'The only great English batsman I know who is an exception to the rule is

Abel, who never uses his legs to guard his wicket.' While as for the
shouldering of arms, Abel himself in 'Some Hints' declared that,
'Far too many off-balls are now left alone which could be safely
cut – particularly late'.

Certainly Abel could on occasion score pretty quickly, not just on
bad wickets. His 160 against Woods and Cambridge University in
1888 was made in four hours, a rate that he bettered in 1896 with his
152 in three and a quarter hours against Leicestershire, including a
century before lunch and prompting *Wisden* to remark that 'never
has Abel played with greater vigour'. Two years later, in the
post-Lord's confrontation of honour with Kortright, his aggregate of
201 against Essex was compiled in a total of four and a quarter
hours, though of course he had his private reasons for not wishing to
hang around. While at Worcester in 1901 he made 96 in as short a
time as eighty-five minutes, 'an innings', according to *Cricket*,
'which for attractiveness could not have been surpassed by any of
the quick scorers'. He was also capable of participating in a run-
chase more profitably than at Cheltenham in 1889. For the South at
the Oval in 1894 he made a half century in almost even time before
the chase was called off as impossible; two years later at Edgbaston
his 33 in forty-five minutes helped to get Surrey home by ten
wickets just before the rain came down; and versus Somerset at the
Oval in 1898, after making 81 in two and a quarter hours in the first
innings, his unbeaten 64 out of 153 for 1 was made in 101 of the
permitted 105 minutes, though *Wisden* did criticize Woods for
'keeping Lionel Palairet on with lobs rather too long'.

Overall, there are no good grounds for regarding Abel as any
more selfish a player than most batsmen. Following rain at home to
Cambridge in 1900, for instance, he 'forced the game so as to get the
best of the wicket in case the sun came out – which it didn't – and hit
up 53 in just over the hour'. Perhaps the last word (if not figure) in
the great debate about Abel as fox or hedgehog should go to *Wisden*'s
summary of his play during that same season: 'He was the same
admirable batsman as ever, full of resources, and, while quite
content to wait for his runs when any difficulties presented themselves, quick to punish the bowling whenever it fell in the least
below the mark.'

How long Abel took to make his decent scores is usually recorded
in the match reports of the period. Between 1881 and 1893, in 125

timed innings, he scored 6,281 runs in 15,174 minutes, working out
at an average of 24.8 runs per hour. The second half of his career
saw a marked increase in pace: 267 timed innings between 1894 and
1904 brought him 18,272 runs in 34,505 minutes, a rate of 31.37 rph.
Or, taking his career as a whole, between 1881 and 1904 he scored,
in 392 timed innings, 24,553 runs in 49,679 minutes (about thirty-
four days), averaging 29.6 rph. One has to turn to Gerald Brodribb's
plum-pudding of a book, *All Round The Wicket* (1951), to see where
29.6 measures on the Richter scale of spectator excitement. In it he
takes the leading batsmen of the previous three-quarters of a century
(omitting Abel) and, on the basis of 'a considerable number of
innings', works out their rates of scoring. In his main list, which
excludes batsmen with a career average of under 25, top is Jessop
on 80 rph, followed by Constantine on 79. The bottom four are
V. M. Merchant on 29 rph, Shrewsbury and B. Mitchell on 28,
and, inevitably, Johnny 'Won't Hit Today' Douglas on 22. Various
others of Abel's contemporaries besides Jessop and Shrewsbury
also feature: 'Very Fast Scoring' Crawford on 61, Trumper on 56,
Ranji on 50, MacLaren on 48, Fry and Jackson on 40, Hayward on
37, and W. G. on 36. Amongst those with a career average of under
25, the four sluggards of Abel's time are the resonant quartet of Hall
on 17, Scotton and Bannerman on 16 and Barlow on 14. From all of
which one may conclude that though not all that slow for a professional, Abel in comparison with the leading amateur batsmen of
his era was batting in a different lane.

One thing, however, that these figures do not reveal is the degree
of acceleration attained in the course of a major innings. According
to Lilley, Abel 'never altered his game or seemed to tire' and
'always played at the end of his innings as if he had just gone in'. On
the basis of the internal timings for fifty-eight of his big scores (most
of course made in his later, quicker-scoring years), this is an assertion
open to some dispute. Abel averaged ninety-four minutes to reach
50, another eighty-nine minutes to attain three figures, and only
fifty minutes to get from 100 to 150. If, however, the innings showed
signs of turning into a real epic, especially a record-making epic,
Abel tended to put the brakes on after 150 and revert to norm. Thus
against Warwickshire in 1897, his first 50 took seventy minutes, his
second eighty, his third sixty, his fourth eighty, and his fifth ninety.
While four years later, for the Players, he scored a century in 145

minutes, went to 150 in another hour, but then took 155 minutes to get from 150 to 247. It was, though, the biggest epic of them all that showed that Lilley had a point: in it Abel scored his first 50 at 37 rph and then went from 50 to 250 at 42 rph, before easing off slightly to 41 rph for the final stretch from 250 to 357. He was not a batsman to put the foot down when he could cruise so effectively.

As a coda to the theme of his rate of scoring, one should perhaps also consider the question of dominance, in other words what proportion of the runs added while he was at the wicket he scored himself. Usually, of course, he scored his runs more slowly than the other main batsmen on the side. Fairly typical was the match at Edgbaston in 1900, when on a somewhat difficult wicket Surrey batted through the last day to ensure a draw: whereas Hayward scored his 127 in three and a half hours, Abel took some five hours over his 'all but faultless' 112. Abel himself once remarked to Bettesworth that 'there is a great temptation to hit when your partner begins to knock the bowling into a cocked hat', but it was a temptation to which he rarely succumbed. Thus in his innings of 357 he maintained his even tenor as Crawford scored a hurricane 129 and dominated a sixth-wicket partnership of 211. Indeed, the eventual total against Somerset of 811 is still the record for the amount of runs added with a single player at the wicket. Abel's career figures in this respect reflect a similar pattern of subordination, though not servile subordination. In 829 innings for which details are available, he scored 30,453 runs out of a total of 68,722 (including extras) added while he was at the wicket, a proportion of 44.3%. As one would expect, he became relatively less subordinate in his later years, with 10,557 runs out of 25,248 (41.8%) up to 1893 being stepped up from 1894 to 19,896 out of 43,474 (45.7%). Interestingly, as an opener in 710 of these innings he scored 44.6% of the runs added, compared to 41.7% in 119 innings as a non-opener – a discrepancy at least partly to be accounted for by the fact that he tended to bat lower down the order in the less productive, and therefore more tentative, early and very late years of his career.

When Abel opened, it is also of some relevance as an additional yardstick of relative dominance to see how many wickets fell before he was out. For the nine times that he carried his bat it has to be assumed for statistical purposes that his would have been the next wicket to fall, an unfairness perhaps roughly balanced out by the non-inclusion of the times that his side won by eight wickets or whatever and he was not out at the end. Anyway, in 688 innings as an opener an average of 1.52 wickets fell at the other end before he was out, an indication of his well-developed limpet qualities, being half a wicket above the long-run statistical 'norm' for an opener of 0.98. Significantly, the average of 1.47 up to 1893 was only marginally bettered in the years from 1894 to 1904, when it was 1.56. In other words, though Abel's individual run-getting figures became vastly better from 1894, his importance as the backbone of Surrey's early batting was much less dramatically enhanced. From which the conclusion is again inescapable that what really made the difference to his leaping annual aggregate from the mid-1890s was the general improvement in the quality of wickets, above all at his beloved Oval.

Ultimately, however, Abel's abiding flaw as a batsman was not his heavy reliance on Apted's prepared wickets, nor his lack of Jessopian qualities, nor even his cross-batted inadequacies against really fast bowling. Trevor, writing in the *Sportsman* in 1899 about Abel's non-appearance in the England sides of that year despite his prolific scoring, put his finger on what that flaw was: 'The question of anxiety has to be considered, and Abel is certainly rather an anxious batsman. He is by no means the only one amongst our great cricketers, but anxiety in a big match seldom helps the man who is troubled with it.' It was a problem which one might have expected to have affected him particularly in his less seasoned years. Discussing the general theme of pre-century anxiety, traditionally the most acute of cricket's tests of nerve, Alcock in an 1893 interview remarked that, 'Abel was several years before he could overcome that nervous feeling just before making a hundred, and it used to take him a very long time to make the needed two or three runs.' In fact, though, the nineties became no less nervous for Abel during his prime than they had been earlier. Despite never actually being out for 99, he is invariably described in match reports as batting with manifest anxiety at this stage of his innings. 'A County Cricketer' had this to say in the *Athletic News* in 1902:

I have asked more than one crack bowler this summer whose wicket he considers the most difficult to get, and the result is a

tie between Abel and Shrewsbury, with a slight preponderance
of opinion in favour of the latter. There is a stonewall air about
the batting of the two that looks for all the world like a
ninety-nine-year lease of the wicket after the first half hour.
But where the Notts professor holds the trump card over the
Guv'nor is in the late forties and nineties. Both are still keen
enough to get the coveted 50 and 100, but the one shows his
keenness by the fidgety batting customary at such a stage, the
other does not, and Bobbie Abel is the one that does. Indeed,
one county bowler told me this summer that the very best time
to get Abel after he has once settled down is in the forties and
nineties, and confessed to me that he almost gave him up once
he had reached the half-century until he was approaching 90!

Why was Abel so regularly unmanned at these two stages? Partly,
of course, because of the same intrinsic reasons that cricketers
always have been, but partly also because of the reason put forward
in *The Jubilee Book* by the two well-known amateur centurions:

> The institution of talent money has cost many a professional
> his wicket in county cricket. Most counties give their repre-
> sentatives a sovereign for every 50 runs they make. Naturally
> this makes them all the more anxious when they approach the
> required totals. That sovereign causes innumerable run-outs
> and rash strokes.

Abel's nerve was also raw if he was in sight of breaking a batting
record, as his jangled performances at the end of the 1900 and 1901
seasons made palpably clear. Or, as *Wisden* recorded about his 250
against Warwickshire in 1897 that surpassed his previous highest
innings of 231: 'He has rarely hit with more sustained vigour, but as
he approached his record score he became very cautious, and took
nearly an hour to make 19 runs.' Abel could even get in a stew about
his 2,000 for the season. In 1897 again, batting for the Players at
Hastings, 'when nearing the desired number he seemed terribly
anxious, and twice nearly ran himself out'. Perhaps Abel would not
have stayed calm anyway, but there is no doubt that in general the
crowd did not help, especially the rather febrile Oval crowd. 'A fact
that aroused the crowd to a high pitch of enthusiasm,' was how the

Sporting Life described the response in 1898 to Abel becoming the first batsman to reach 2,000 for the season. In an era preoccupied with records of all sorts, Abel's nervousness merely reflected the popular obsession. Moreover, the home crowd desperately wanted their favourite to do well – and Abel more than many sporting heroes was near enough to them in spirit to be fully conscious of that burden of hopeful expectancy. One such moment of what must have been almost cathartic empathy came when he was on 99 in Surrey's first match against the Australians in 1896. Amidst the 'pardonable anxiety' of the crowd, 'Jones bowled him two overs with the field crouching around close in, and Abel never attempted to hit'. Finally Abel reached the landmark and ' a huge shout went up' from the ring. One more spell on the rack was at last over.

Not everyone, there is no denying, was a fully paid-up member of the Abel appreciation society. 'A Country Vicar', for instance, 'always maintained he was overrated', thereby joining the ranks of Lyttelton and 'An Old Cambridge Blue'. Spofforth in 1902 did not consider him one of the three best English batsmen, while Frank Iredale rated the Governor-General above the Guv'nor. In his memoirs published in 1920 he wrote of Macartney: 'Considering his inches, I doubt if the world ever had a more brilliant batsman. He played with a straighter bat and was far more brilliant than ever Bobby Abel was. In negotiating fast bumpy ones, he was a greater man than either Abel or [Syd] Gregory.'

There was, however, an arguably even stronger dissenting lobby from these and similar views on Abel's overall merits (or otherwise) as a batsman. Trumble's testimony, expressed in 1899, was categorical: 'Our fellows on the '96 tour regarded him as the best batsman in England on all wickets, and Ranji was batting exceptionally well then. Abel has such a wonderful eye.' Fellow-professionals, aware where the proof of the pudding lay, were especially appreciative of his qualities. 'Abel plays in a style which, whatever critics may think of it, stands him nevertheless in a very good stead,' asserted Albert Ward in a 1900 anthology edited by T. C. Collings. While when Walter Mead of Essex was asked in 1904 which batsman over the years had given him most trouble, he replied: 'I think I should place Abel first, when he was in his prime. He always seemed to me more difficult to get out than anyone else.' Jephson, Surrey's equivalent to Fry as a leading amateur who also wrote perceptively on the game, agreed with Mead: 'Say what you like, this Bob of ours, as the people love to call him, is the one man I would select for certainty of defence and the one man I would choose for certainty of runs.' Yet it was a certainty of a very special, idiosyncratic sort. Bettesworth, in one of his pieces on Abel, quoted a northern spectator (presumably from Lancashire rather than Yorkshire) as he watched the runs being steadily piled up against his own team: 'Look at him. He stands there with his bat all cock-eyed, and he moves about like a cat on hot bricks, and yet the little beggar is one of the finest batsmen in the world. Confound him!'

Abel certainly put the runs in the book over the years, and on good wickets many bowlers knew despair in their hearts as the long day's play wore on, but for the spectators it was rather different. Cardus made the point perfectly:

> Bobby Abel came closer to the affections of the Oval crowd than Hayward ever could because of Hayward's abnormal excellence of technique and his generally magisterial air. Abel looked like a typical Cockney; moreover, he played with a cross bat and suggested during his longest and most substantial innings a mortal fallibility which could be felt and shared by one and all.

Ranji/Fry in *The Jubilee Book* may have reckoned Strawyard to be 'the best and soundest bat on the side', but the warmest sympathies of the Ovalites were always with the serio-comic Cain.

Chapter Five

IN THE FIELD

I was in the Pavilion and heard his cheery voice. 'Come and sit here, I want to talk to you about that little Abel,' and *more suo* he was very enthusiastic about his watchfulness at short-slip and his earnest cricket, for Abel was selected by him three years ago as the best of a large batch of colts who answered the invitation to come to the Oval as aspirants to fame. Abel was put on to bowl, and Mr Grimston said, 'Now that is all nonsense – he is only a common village bowler.' My reply was, 'I will bet sixpence he gets a chance before three overs,' and the words were hardly out of my mouth when the ball went full into long-on's hands. 'By Jove! you are right,' said Mr Grimston, 'I must watch that fellow,' and after he had seen another over his remark was, 'He pitches a *good* length, he *can* bowl.'

SUCH WERE THE appreciative words of 'an old cricketer', in a letter sent to *Cricket* in 1884 soon after Grimston's death. They remind one that when Abel first came to the Oval he made as much of an impression by his fielding and bowling as by his batting. Twenty-six wickets in two Colts matches in May 1881, followed in his first-class debut by twice dismissing William Oscroft, was a fair start, even though he had come from Southwark Park primarily as a batsman. He did not do much with the ball in 1882 or 1883, but the next year he took 5 for 34 against Leicestershire (in a non-first-class match) and finished the season with performances of 3 for 7 against Yorkshire and an analysis against Sussex that at one point read 16–11–6–1. Overs were of course four-balls long until 1889, when they became five and remained so until the introduction in 1900 of the modern six-ball over. Abel also turned in a couple of notable sets of figures in 1885: 34–20–39–3 in the second innings at Sheffield and 54–27–59–4 in the second innings of the home match with Notts.

It was becoming increasingly clear, though, that his real potential lay in his batting, and from the mid-1880s his bowling became secondary, as perhaps it always had been in his own mind. 340 overs was the most he ever bowled in a season, in 1887 when Roller, Jones and Beaumont were all unavailable towards the end, and the 31 wickets he took in both 1892 and 1896 represented his highest annual crop. In his first-class career as a whole he took 254 wickets at an average of 24.18. The figure usually given is 263, a discrepancy probably to be explained by the usual non-adjustment of the less important career records to the fact of matches subsequently being demoted to second-class status.

Abel never bowled in a Test match, only occasionally in representative fixtures, and took but one first-class wicket on tour: Knill of South Australia, caught at point, was his victim. He did, however, bowl quite often in the country matches, in 1891–92 even taking 12 for 61 against Twenty-Two of Bairnsdale. At home, Surrey's front-line bowling from the mid-1880s to the mid-1890s was usually formidable enough to require him to be only an inter-mittent change bowler, while when that bowling went into decline around the turn of the century Abel himself was no longer up to long spells. Nevertheless, he did possess something of a d'Oliveira-like reputation for his ability to break up stubborn partnerships: thus in 1886 Walker and Scott were apparently settling in for Middlesex, but Abel in his first over got Scott caught behind and, 'having achieved the object for which he was put on, at once retired in favour of Lohmann'; while in 1897, after the final Hampshire wicket had added 35, 'Abel was put on to get the last man out', and within four balls duly obliged. Or in Shuter's grateful words, he was 'an excellent set off to all other classes of bowling, used his head well, and was instrumental in getting his side out of many an awkward fix'.

According to Pridham, Abel 'rather fancied himself as a bowler'; but Dorey was probably more accurate when he noted in his preface to the reminiscences that Abel regarded his bowling as 'tosh'. What was this bowling in fact like? 'He bowls slow round-arm, with rather a low delivery, and at times gets considerable work on from the off,' was *Cricket*'s summary of it in 1885, while Fry in 1899 referred to his 'high-tossed slows, with a view to catches in the country'. The two fullest descriptions of his bowling were both by people who had faced it. The writer of the 1884 letter to *Cricket* vouchsafed person-ally for Abel's merits:

> I have taken him out to play in a good match in the country, have seen him bowl occasionally in London, and have had him to bowl to me with a shilling on the wicket, so I *ought* to know

something about him, and I have *no* hesitation in saying that he is one of the most deceptive change bowlers we have, because it *looks* such rubbish, but he can pitch a ball on a sixpence almost, and the ball gets up *very* quick and cuts across, and he almost always gets a chance at once.

Bettesworth, who in 1882 for Sussex had been one of Abel's earliest first-class scalps, offered a few thoughts about Abel's bowling in the course of his 1904 profile:

I have often wondered why he has not been more successful as a bowler, for he used to be very awkward to deal with when he first went on. But he looks 'so damned simple' that captains may perhaps have been afraid to put him on. He used to have a big break, and although he was uncommonly slow, the ball came so quickly off the pitch that many a batsman was deceived by it; of course, as with all other bowlers, this quickness off the pitch gradually became less noticeable. But even now, Abel would possibly puzzle many a good batsman just sufficiently long enough for him to get a wicket; he was never a man to keep on for any length of time, except on the rarest occasions, when batsmen seemed afflicted by a wild yearning to go home to the pavilion.

Lemming tendencies or otherwise of the batsmen, deviation as such was no problem. 'Abel was able to make the ball do a good deal, as he often can,' the *Sporting Life* reported about his bowling against Kent in 1896. And, moreover, he could apparently get the ball to go either way, not just breaking back from the off. For as C. E. Horner, Surrey's amateur bowler, recalled to Bettesworth: 'I remember Abel bowling W. G. at Clifton with a ball which came round his legs. It was a very slow one indeed, and broke ever so much. Abel can do a good break down, and he was so much pleased with his feat that he gave us an impromptu performance.' The season was 1884, Grace had made 66, and any jig of triumph that Abel danced was, in the circumstances, understandable.

In terms of how Abel got his 254 wickets, the breakdown shows that 145 of them were caught, 68 bowled, 24 stumped, 13 lbw, and 4 hit wicket. A fairly typical catch off his bowling occurred at Hove in

Probably *v* Derbyshire at the Oval, 1895

1889 when, in the only over he bowled in the innings, he achieved the break that Surrey needed by getting Brann caught at long-on, after earlier in the over conceding two fours to him. There are several similar examples: for instance, A. O. Jones at the Oval in 1893 'drove Abel for four, but in a rash attempt to repeat the stroke he made a faulty hit, and was easily caught at cover-point'; while three years later Derbyshire's Davidson, after 61 stolid runs, 'was at length tempted to hit out at Abel, and lifting the ball to long-off, Hayward brought off a grand catch'. Not all catches, though, were in the middle to distant regions. At Clifton in 1884, in what was clearly Abel's lucky match, Brain 'was driving a ball when he accidentally shied away his bat, which went to square leg, whilst the ball was secured at point'. Indeed, as many as 47 of the 115 detailed catches off his bowling were taken by either wicket-keeper or slip, a fact perhaps partly explained by the *Sporting Life*'s mention of how in 1896 Hampshire's D. A. Steele was caught behind 'off a fastish ball'.

As for the 24 stumpings, few can have given the square-leg umpire any problem. 'Scott jumped out to drive Abel, and, missing the ball, was easily stumped,' an episode in the away match with Middlesex in 1893 was the standard fare. The previous year, a North versus South match had seen Abel lay one of his more sophisticated traps. After Gunn had been taking guard a foot outside his crease to face Lohmann, the *Hastings and St Leonards Times* described what happened when Abel came on: 'A rather novel sight was now witnessed, Gunn keeping to his long block, and Abel delivering the ball about two yards before reaching the crease.' And: 'Abel proved too wily for Gunn. He pitched a wide ball, which Wood snatched up and whipped off the bails before the great Notts player could regain his ground.' At least Gunn was dismissed in a festival context, unlike his even greater colleague at the Oval in 1896: 'When Abel came on with his slows, Shrewsbury lost his judgement and patience, jumped out to drive, missed the ball, and was easily stumped.'

It was much the same story with Abel's bowled victims, who only rarely lost their wickets playing defensively. In 1896, versus Lancashire, Abel did 'beat Baker with a simple-looking ball that broke in suddenly', but much more common was the self-inflicted fate in 1885 of the same county's Hildyard, who 'ran several yards out of his ground to a ball, missed it, and was bowled'. At Derby in 1887 Disney 'struck across at a ball from Abel and was bowled', a rather less humiliating dismissal than that of McGahey at the Oval ten years later, when, on 94, he 'jumped in to a ball from Abel and made a wild attempt to hit', only of course to hear, some time afterwards, the familiar rattle. But the dismissal of this sort that Abel himself recalled with evident pleasure occurred at Bramall Lane as early as 1885:

> I bowled Ulyett a slow, pitched up wide of the off stump. The burly Yorkshireman, jumping out, made a tremendous lunge at the ball, missed it, and was bowled. Walking from the crease in evident disgust at missing such a soft ball, he remarked to me, 'If ah'd hit ut, ut wd ha' gone to Lunnon.'

In the same fixture three years earlier Ulyett had almost hit him into the English Channel: two consecutive balls went soaring over the rails, the first of which 'struck a lady, and she had to be assisted to a private room in the pavilion'. An even bigger hitter of Abel's slows was Nottinghamshire's Flowers, who in 1883 drove him out of Trent Bridge for six and then in 1892, in the epochal match at the Oval, dispatched him on to the roof of the covered stand. Inevitably Abel was at times expensive: three overs at Taunton in 1896 cost him 29, including five fours by Tyler; in a festival match at Hastings in 1900 he clocked up a half-century in only five overs; and in 1901 Warwickshire's Kinneir took 16 off one of his overs, though the following day Abel had him stumped. He was in general, however, reasonably economical: each six balls he bowled cost him an average of 2.62 runs, an average which was especially reasonable for a bowler who was often reckoned to buy his wickets. The *Sportsman* in 1883 referred to 'the youngster Abel being especially dead on the "sticks"' in the home match with Yorkshire in 1883, while against the same opponents four years later he opened Surrey's weakened bowling with a string of five maidens. And just occasionally, in addition to breaking a partnership and/or keeping the runs down, he could actually be devastating. His career-best figures were 24.2–16–15–6 in 1887, on a treacherous, rain-affected wicket on the last day at the Oval against Derbyshire, but he returned several other notable analyses: 11–2–18–3 on another rain-affected Oval wicket against Gloucestershire in 1891, 8–1–29–5 to take Surrey to victory against Somerset in 1892, and 28–9–55–6 in a similarly match-winning performance versus Sussex in 1894.

But perhaps his most cherishable hour as a bowler occurred at Lord's in 1896 when, on a badly broken-up pitch, his match figures of 6 for 46 helped Surrey to an innings victory over Middlesex. After taking two wickets in the first innings, he 'received an encouraging cheer' as he went on to bowl at the start of the second innings, got O'Brien caught at slip with his second ball, and proceeded to bowl unchanged with Richardson. Over the next few weeks he several times opened the Surrey bowling, including on the first morning against Notts in front of a crowd of over 30,000, but never with quite the same success. Thereafter his bowling gradually waned, though at Chesterfield in 1899 he took 4 for 17 and the following year, in the home match against Kent, picked up 4 for 21. His fourth victim on that latter occasion was the young Blythe, who earlier in the match, 'to the dismay of the crowd', had bowled him for 2. There is no doubt which of the two bowlers would have derived the greater satisfacton from their respective successes.

Curiously, most of the great golden-age batsmen in England, with the notable exception of Fry, fell to Abel's lures at one time or another. In fact, Abel's only undoubted superior amongst his fellow-professional batsmen, Shrewsbury, was out to him no less than three times: the stumping of 1896 had been preceded by a caught and bowled in 1885 and was followed by a contentious LBW in 1899. 'It was Louis Hall's decision, and gave rise to a lot of grumbling amongst the Notts men, as Shrewsbury himself, as well as his partner, Jones, declared emphatically that he played the ball.' Earlier in 1899 Abel caught and bowled Ranji, 'from a ball which he went in to hit but got only half hold of'. His score at that time was 197, but the event still apparently occasioned 'the almost delirious joy of Mr Key'. Another impressive victim, at least on paper, was MacLaren, who as Lancashire batted out the final afternoon of the match at the Oval in 1898 was caught by Brockwell 'from a lofty straight drive'.

Can one perhaps conclude, on the basis of these famous scalps and his career figures generally, that Abel was under-bowled? 'Some good judges,' according to *Cricket* in 1885, 'are inclined to think he might be more often utilized with advantage.' One of them

was almost certainly Gale, for as the *Sporting Life* noted after the
Sussex match in 1894: 'Bobby Abel's capital analysis will no doubt
please the heart of the "Old Buffer", who years ago was always
declaiming against Shuter for not giving Abel more opportunities
with the ball.' While as late as 1901, as Yorkshire played out a draw
with Surrey at Bradford, there was at least one man who took a
similar view: 'I often think "Shrimp" was at fault for not putting on
Abel,' Lord Hawke wrote in his reminiscences a long time afterwards. Yet overall, whatever the debatable justice of these opinions,
it is hard not to feel that it was for the best that Abel was bowled as
relatively sparingly as he was. He may have been stronger than he
looked, but he was hardly built in the mould of the durable all-
rounder. To have become a front-line bowler would surely have
adversely affected his batting – and that he never regarded as 'tosh'.

The Times in its obituary of Abel eloquently described his early
struggles as a professional batsman:

> Such skill as he then possessed he had acquired at Southwark
> Park, without the advantage of any particular coaching, and
> naturally he took some time to accustom himself to first-class
> company. But he was very keen on the game, and long before
> his batting developed he won the good opinion of some of the
> authorities at the Oval by his smartness in the field.

This time it is Gale who supplies a relevant anecdote, comple-
menting the one about Abel's accurate bowling during the 1881 trial
games. He told it in the course of an interview with Bettesworth
in 1893 in which he was asked about remarkable performances in
village matches:

> The match was Mitcham versus Sutton, on a Bank Holiday.
> Sutton had 14 runs to get, and had three wickets to go down.
> They had got seven of these when George Jones was put on
> with orders to bowl his hardest. The first ball went towards
> Abel, at short-slip, who was then quite unknown. He made a
> jump, caught it with his left hand, and rolled over on his back.
> The next ball also came somewhere near him. He sprang
> up like a spider and just got it. The next ball went to the

wicket-keeper, who was standing back. He succeeded in partly stopping it, and it went over his head into the hands of Abel, who had got round him like a shadow. I wrote particulars of this to Fred Burbidge, who was a great advocate for Abel.

The exact date of this episode is uncertain, as is why Abel should have been playing for Mitcham, but that he was full of youthful agility is not left in doubt. Indeed, Bettesworth himself in 1904 remembered him 'in the old days' as being 'as quick as a cat in the field, so that he could reach balls which many a tall man would have allowed to pass by'. In the course of his first-class career, Abel in fact held 547 catches (cf. the figure of 492 sometimes given), of which the position in which he took them can be identified for all but 121. Easily top is slip, where he took at least 314 catches and was usually stationed until the mid-1890s. It is followed by point with 21 catches, himself as bowler with 13, mid-off with 12, cover-point and long field with 11 each, mid-on with 9, long-on and long-off with 8 each, third man with 7, wicket-keeper with 6, extra mid-off and extra cover-point with 2 each, and extra-cover and deep square leg with 1 each. From which figures alone it is pretty clear, amongst other things, that he was not 'the last of the specialist mid-ons'.

Grace's 1899 book of cricketing reminiscences recalled how 'when Lohmann and Abel were in the slips together it was terribly difficult for a batsman to get a ball away in that direction'. It was Lohmann who really made the position of cover-slip, where he seemed able, as Grace's earlier cricket book put it, 'to get to everything within six feet of him'. Hayward in 1903 described him as 'the best slip that I ever saw in the Surrey eleven', while in Altham's words he was 'as great a slip-fielder as the world has known'. Abel, however, was in his own right a fully worthy member of the Surrey 'box'. *Cricket* in 1885 asserted that 'at short-slip he has no superior at the present time', a theme that the *Athletic News* took up the following year:

Little Bobby Abel at short-slip is a veritable demon. That catch with which he dismissed Walter Read in the second innings of the Gentlemen at the Oval was a clinker. In this position Abel, despite his short stature, has few, if any, superiors. He is as good there as Shrewsbury is at point, which is saying a good deal.

And at the end of the 1891 season the *Sporting Life* even noted how Abel at slip 'fairly rivalled Lohmann as a fieldsman', than which there was no higher praise. The most catches that he ever took at slip in a first-class match was at Derby in 1884, when at least five of the six that he held were in that position; though at Leicester in 1890, in a second-class match, he took six catches at slip in the first innings alone, including the first five on the card.

Possessing the qualities of a jack-in-the-box was the key to his success as a slipper. Thus in 1882 O'Shaughnessy for Kent was 'finely taken by Abel, who managed to secure the ball, only just clear of the ground, after it had travelled just out of the reach of the wicket-keeper, Pooley'. In the following season Lord Harris, in the same fixture, was 'cleverly caught at slip by Abel, who just got his left hand on to the ball', while Cambridge University's Mansfield was 'brilliantly caught off a late hand-cut'. In 1885 Oxford's Brain was 'secured in the slips by Abel, who effected the capture with one hand high up'; and three years later Trott, for the Australians against Surrey, was out to 'a marvellous catch at slip by Abel, who took the ball whilst turning round'.

Inevitably, though, life in the slips was not all swallow-dives and back-slapping. On Bank Holiday Monday at the Oval in 1882, Barnes, after he had been batting for a few minutes, 'should have been caught at slip, Abel touching the ball rather high up with his right hand', and he then went on to make 130 out of Nottingham-shire's first-day 352 for 2. Three years later, at Liverpool, Briggs took advantage of being twice dropped by Abel at slip to make 186. And at Cheltenham in 1892 the biggest one of all got away, when W. G. sent up a skier, any of the three slips 'might have caught it', and Abel, with misguided confidence, decided it was his. One can almost hear the rather squeaky laugh.

Abel experienced some particularly critical moments at slip during Test matches against Australia. In the 1888 series Barnes tended to take the position, but could not be there always – and in the first innings at the Oval, Edwards 'was badly let off by Abel fielding at slip to Barnes, the "midget" allowing the ball to drop between his hands in endeavouring to hug it to his stomach'. Subsequently in the series, however, Abel took two slip catches, though at Old Trafford he missed Trott low down off 'what would have been a remarkable catch had he made it'. Three and a half years later in Australia he generally fielded well at slip, taking four catches in the series, but at Sydney had a terrible few minutes that undeniably took away some of the glitter from his marvellous batting earlier in the match. In Australia's second innings Lyons had reached 49 when he was twice missed by Abel at slip in one over from Sharpe. According to the *Australasian*, 'The first was easy, the second sudden, but Abel dropped both of them, and for a time had to endure many reproachful looks from his side.' Probably for quite a long time, in that Lyons went on to make a match-winning 134.

Rather less traumatic were his outings at slip in the Tests of 1896, even though he had by this time more or less stopped fielding there for Surrey. The match at Lord's featured a chase rather than a catch:

> One of the most amusing incidents of the game was the effort of Abel to retrieve the ball after it had knocked off the bail on Trumble's wicket. Under the impression that it was a hit or a bye, Abel sped with the utmost rapidity after the ball, and the crowd, waking up to the situation, applauded heartily, while the English team also entered into the fun of the thing. Amidst thunders of applause, Abel gathered the ball when going at top speed and returned it beautifully to the wicket-keeper.

And according to the *Morning Leader*, 'it was some minutes before the spectators had done laughing'; while Abel himself later told a reporter that 'I didn't know it had touched the stumps, I never heard it'. In the Second Test, at Old Trafford, Iredale made 108 on the first day and *The Times* reported: 'Between the seventies and eighties he had almost a life at the hands of Abel, at short slip. Abel used to be a certain catch in this position; but the best of cricketers will often fail.' Abel as a top cricketer must have read this soft impeachment, to judge by a passage in the following day's *Star*: 'Abel denies that he missed catching Iredale yesterday. He says the ball did not come to him, and Phillips, the umpire, corroborates the Surrey midget.'

All this, however, was forgotten by the time of the Oval decider. On the third day McKibbin by 'plucky hitting' in a hopeless cause took Australia's score from 25 for 9 up to 44, until at 1.40 Abel 'caught him most brilliantly at slip with one hand' (his only slip

catch of the season) and clinched the series. Travers recalled Abel
'collaring the ball and in one and the same movement making a
dash with it to the pavilion', an alacrity to be explained by the
custom of the player who finished with the match ball being allowed
to keep it. And as Abel himself recollected: 'As I passed in at the
wicket-gate, Mr Arthur Duke, of Messrs Duke & Son, of Tonbridge,
offered me £5 for the ball. This I refused, as I did subsequently an
offer of £6 by George Lohmann.' He presumably put it somewhere
safe before he went up on the balcony.

In an article in the 1893 *Wisden*, 'A Few Words on Fielding',
Lohmann paid tribute to Abel's all-round ability as a fielder: 'I have
seen him make some very fine catches near the boundary, and I
can only say that unfortunately there are not many Abels about.'
Several instances from match reports confirm Lohmann's praise. At
Lord's in 1883, Paravicini 'drove Horner high to long-off, where
Abel held the ball, and he had to accept his dismissal'. Two years
later, for the Players of the South in his first representative match,
he caught his county colleague Bowden with 'a well-judged catch at
long-field-on'. And in 1889, for the South at Old Trafford, he took 'a
fine catch close on the rails' to dismiss Sugg. He also seems in his
prime as a fieldsman to have had a good arm: in the Third Test in
1888 Trott was run out when Abel 'threw the ball smartly in from
the long field'. He may well have had a penchant for escaping from
his regular position at slip, for when he collided with Wood in the
deep in 1884 in the match against the Colts, he should not really
have been there at all. As Wood recalled:

> Abel, who was fielding at short-slip, asked Mr Read, the
> captain, to let him go into the long field. A burning desire came
> over me to also go out, and Mr Read was kind enough to let me
> keep Abel company. I was on the on side, and Abel was deep
> long-off. One of the Colts hit a ball up, and we both ran for the
> catch . . .

Occasionally, his lack of practice in the country could betray him
in other ways, usually in representative matches when someone
else had taken his normal spot. 'The fielding was good, with the
exception of Abel, who has been so long accustomed to working in
the slips that it seemed quite out of place to put him in the long

field,' the *Sportsman* observed about the Players at Lord's in 1886, in the course of which match Robertson skied one to the on and 'should have been caught, but Abel could not see the ball'. While at the Oval six years later, also for the Players, his fortunes were mixed: 'Hedley, in attempting to drive, was finely caught deep behind the bowler by Abel, who jumped and reached the ball in its flight with his right hand. It was a superb catch, and went some little way towards redeeming the many mistakes that player had made in the field.'

Abel usually had a safe pair of hands in the middle range: in the home match with Notts in 1884, fielding as substitute for C. W. Wright, he apologetically caught Roller at mid-off; on his Test debut 'a smart catch at mid-on' accounted for Worrall; and in 1889 Sugg for the North at Hastings 'succumbed to a catch at third man by Abel, the feat being greeted with loud applause by the spectators'. Close to the wicket, he did not often leave the slips, though again in the First Test of 1888, 'Edwards put one up very hotly to Abel at short leg', where he failed to take the catch but 'threw in the ball beautifully to the opposite end, where Briggs, had he only taken the ball at the first attempt, could have put the wicket down'.

During the course of two seasons, however, persistent hand injuries to Wood saw Abel among others being drafted in as Surrey's emergency wicket-keeper. In 1887 he 'officiated smartly behind the sticks' at Old Trafford and later in the riotous Notts match caught Attewell behind the wicket, but between times had his problems at home to Oxford: 'Little Abel was requisitioned to put on the pads and gloves. 35 extras tell that there was a screw loose here, but it was not thought worthwhile to have a long-stop on'. Five years later he was again pressed into service: at Oxford, standing 'several yards back' to Lockwood, Lohmann and Sharpe, he 'acquitted himself most creditably'; and soon afterwards he started to do the same against Gloucestershire until W. G. intervened, saying that 'he did not want to see a good little batsman like Bobby Abel injured' and giving permission for the substitute fielder, Watts, to act as wicket-keeper. In one of the matches the following season he did keep wicket 'for some little time, until Marshall arrived', but in 1894, when Surrey were again short of a keeper on a particular day, it was Jephson who did the job, acknowledging the fact that Abel's hands had become too precious to be treated carelessly.

In his latter years he still fielded occasionally in the slips, for
instance at Portsmouth in 1898 compensating for his duck against
Heseltine by taking four catches in his old position, in addition to
two at mid-off. But if from the mid-1890s he was reckoned no longer
to have the reflexes and agility to be a regular slip, he was certainly
not yet the liability in the field that might be deduced from an
article in *Wisden Cricket Monthly* in January 1981 on productive
single strokes:

> Clem Hill, playing for the Australians against Surrey at the
> Oval, hit Tom Richardson for seven, eight, and nine in two
> consecutive overs. The fielder responsible for the overthrows
> was Bobby Abel, who was so winded by his exertions that on
> the third occasion he did not retrieve the ball until the fifth run
> was almost completed. Not surprisingly his throw eluded the
> wicket-keeper and went to the boundary.

Almost certainly, though, Hill was not the batsman and Abel not
the fielder in this episode from 1896. According to the *Sporting Life*,
'When Hill came in Gregory increased his score with marvellous
rapidity, cutting Brockwell for four, and having a cut for five off
Richardson increased by a wild throw-in by Brockwell and some
misfielding by Leveson-Gower to nine.'
During these turn-of-the-century years Abel fielded with success
in a variety of positions: at home to Middlesex in 1899, 'running
backwards from mid-off', he 'brought off a wonderful catch high
up'; at Leeds in 1897, with Richardson bowling in front of an
enormous Jubilee crowd, Jackson off the second ball of the match
'was finely caught at third man, Abel holding the ball at the second
attempt'; and at the Oval in 1898 Hallows was 'out to a clever
running catch, Abel crossing the ball at long-off and holding it'. The
Lakerism about him as a specialist mid-on probably derives from
the crisp final paragraph of the 1902 pen portrait in *Vanity Fair*: 'He
is the father of nine children; and he can field at mid-on.'
Though he did field sometimes at mid-on, increasingly the
positions he made a speciality out of were point and (to a lesser
extent) cover-point. Point at this time was a position in retreat in
more senses than one, for according to W. J. Ford in the *Athletic
News* in 1902, 'nowadays the weakling or the greybeard goes there,

and men's reputations depend on their prowess in the slips'. Nevertheless, it was a position in which Abel favourably impressed the critics, taking a series of fine catches, none perhaps better than at Bradford in 1901, when 'from a very hard cut Denton was brilliantly caught at point by Abel, who held the ball with the right hand'. And in 1904 Bettesworth was moved to write that 'even now at point he often quite easily takes a ball which would frighten many a younger man out of his wits'. Moreover, he was for a while distinctly fleet of foot in that position. In the home match with Derbyshire in 1899, after Hulme had been 'cleverly caught by the Guv'nor at point', Higson 'played a ball somewhat wide in the direction of Abel, who gathered the ball like lightning and threw down the amateur's wicket'.

Inevitably by the end, quite apart from his eye troubles, his speed was fading and his hands softening. 'At the beginning of the season thick kid gloves might be worn, as they are by Abel and Shrewsbury,' Benson and Miles informed their readers about fielding in 1903. The sort of mistake he was making that he might not have some years earlier was perhaps at Edgbaston in 1901, when Devey, the Aston Villa captain, was 'missed at deep mid-on by Abel, who came forward half a dozen yards, whereas had he kept to his original position he might have brought off an easy catch', though it is worth adding that in the same fixture the following season he caught Devey off a skier, running in from mid-on to short leg. His fielding seems to have been particularly faulty for the Players at the Oval in 1900, highlighted by two episodes on the morning of the second day: each time Jones hit Trott for four, with first 'Abel, at long-on, not catching sight of the ball until too late to field it' and then 'Abel, at mid-on, letting the ball pass between his legs'. While at Taunton in 1901, according to *The Times*, 'The Surrey fielding was anything but clean, Abel and Richardson frequently being at fault over their ground work.'

It was in such a context that Bettesworth in the same year remarked that 'if his fielding was half as good as his batting he would always be among the first three or four men picked to represent England'; and that when he was recalled in 1902 a question-mark continued to hang over his selection. In the event, he had a good match in the field at Bramall Lane: in the first innings Gregory 'chopped hard at a ball from Barnes and was very finely caught at point, Abel snatching up the ball in great style'; and in the second, with Hill batting, the local paper referred to 'a hard cut that a brilliant stop by Abel at cover-point kept down to a single'. Ashley-Cooper's post-match verdict was therefore naturally sanguine – 'in some quarters it was felt his fielding might handicap the side, but his activity at Sheffield should end all such surmises' – yet unfortunately premature. Apart from a reference to Rhodes being 'cut by Duff for three, the stroke misfielded by Abel', there is no direct evidence of any inadequate fielding by him at Old Trafford, but the indications are clear enough. As the *Sporting Life* put it in its analysis of the team that was chosen for the Fifth Test:

> Jessop gets his place essentially for his fielding. Quite one of the features of the Manchester match was the ease with which the Australians scored singles for strokes just in front of the wicket. Had Jessop been at extra mid-off or cover-point the Australians would never have dared to attempt such short runs.

Three small runs for the batsmen, but a giant step for a fielder aged 44 years and 238 days as he trod the Test arena for the last time.

Abel, like all the professionals of his era, is not remembered as a captain. He captained Surrey once, in 1894 in the absence of Key and despite the presence of Jephson, comfortably defeating Essex by an innings and 261 runs. He also in 1902 captained the Players of England versus the Australians at the Oval in something of a non-match, though it proved to be his swansong as a top-flight cricketer. According to *The Times*, he 'made out a well-judged order'. Otherwise, his experience as a first-class captain was confined to captaining the Players against the Gentlemen, which he did thirteen times between 1894 and 1902: eight times at the Oval, four times at Lord's, and once at Hastings. He did so in the context of a fairly derogatory conventional wisdom:

> Few professional cricketers (it is a well-known fact) make good captains. For the last twenty-five years the Players have always been seriously handicapped by the want of a good captain, though Shrewsbury and Gunn may be exceptions.

Bowlers are kept on maiden after maiden without the faintest chance of a wicket, no originality of attack is ever attempted, and altogether the captaincy is usually bad.

A. G. Steel's words in 1904 were echoed at about the same time by Lyttelton:

In the matter of generalship, or the managing of a side, professionals have hitherto shown very little skill. The professionals themselves would probably prefer to be led by an amateur. George Parr, Daft, Emmett, Alfred Shaw, and Abel have at different times acted as captains, but none are to be compared to Messrs V. E. Walker, A. N. Hornby, J. Shuter, and MacLaren.

Captaining the Players, Abel was certainly not without a cautious streak. At the Oval in 1899 he batted through until almost half past three on the second day as the Players compiled 647; while at Lord's two years later 'it was curious, when Jessop went in, to see five men in the country for a fast bowler like Hirst'. The only time, though, that he was seriously criticized on tactical grounds was also in that 1901 match, when the *Sporting Life* took him to task:

Abel managed his bowling in quite an eccentric fashion. He very properly started with Rhodes and Hirst, but curiously enough he had Rhodes on at the pavilion wicket. Having regard to the slope, one would have imagined that the bowlers would have been better suited had they changed ends. Stranger still when only 19 runs had been scored Hirst was taken off, while Rhodes, though a chance of stumping had been missed off him, was taken off with the score at 23.

Indeed, Abel seems to have been the very opposite of the professional captain depicted by Steel who unimaginatively used the same bowlers over after over. At the Oval in 1894 he twice tried double changes as Grace and Jackson put on 94 for the first wicket; and five years later there, as he tried to winkle out the Gentlemen twice in a day and a half, he made 'numerous bowling changes', including bringing on the Derbyshire wicket-keeper Storer, who

took three wickets in the second innings as the batsmen vainly
strove for a draw. The following week, at Lord's, even *The Times*
was full of praise for his captaincy: Abel 'made the most of his
bowling and the field was generally well placed', so that 'on a
perfectly true pitch a fine batting team were prevented from reaching an even normal rate of scoring', managing on the first day a
derisory 373 for 6 in six hours of cricket. And according to Trevor in
the *Sportsman*, 'Abel always had his team in hand, and there was
never a sign of disorganization in the field.' That he did have his
team in hand, even though he had not originally been selected to
play in the match and was captain only in the absence of Gunn and
Shrewsbury, was clearly demonstrated on the second evening: with
forty-five minutes of play left and Bradley raring to go, Abel was
not one of the batsmen who emerged from the Pavilion as the
Players followed on.

The following year, 1900, the situation at the same stage of the
match was distinctly similar, though this time the Players were
preparing for the fourth innings of the match. Abel himself told the
story:

> I was captain of the professionals, and had been rather badly
> knocked about by Jessop's bowling in the first innings, so I
> asked Carpenter on the Tuesday evening to get his pads on
> and go in first. For some reason or other he refused, which
> somewhat vexed J. T. Brown. 'I'll go in first, Bob, if he won't,'
> said Brown.

On such occasions the Players' dressing-room at Lord's cannot
have been the easiest place in the world in which to pull rank.

Chapter Six

A PRO'S LOT

The amateurs in the two teams were out grouse shooting during the morning, and shortly after they arrived on the ground the decision was arrived at to abandon play for the day.

THUS WAS LOST, after heavy overnight rain, the second day of Surrey's match with Derbyshire at Glossop in 1902: the amateurs presumably returned to their sport, while Abel, not out 87, continued to practise patiently in front of the mirror in his hotel room. The social divide between the two classes of cricketer barely narrowed in his time, with separate everything still the usual order of the day: luncheon-rooms, dressing-rooms, even entrances on to the playing area. It was not until the 1890s that it became common for the clubs even to provide the professionals with lunch, as a result invariably driving them to the bar as the only place where they could hope to find something to eat. When in 1890 Surrey played at Canterbury, festive hospitality was naturally dispensed to the amateurs, but according to the *Athletic News*, the professionals 'were left to shift for themselves, and thought themselves lucky to get a bit of bread and cheese'. And a year later the situation was no better, for Surrey's committee passed a resolution expressing its 'regret that proper arrangements were not made for the professional members of the eleven in the Kent match at Canterbury'. No doubt an under-nourished Guv'nor never really had a chance of compiling big scores on that particular ground. As for the dressing-room apartheid, there were occasional hints of rebellion, as in 1892. The *Athletic News* again gave the details:

A portion of the pavilion on the Taunton ground is usually reserved for amateurs, there being separate accommodation for the professionals. The Lancashire, Surrey, and other county professionals have confined themselves to the quarters of the paid players, but the Notts men all dressed together, and came out of the 'gentlemen's pavilion', while the two Somerset pros were left alone in their glory.

According to the same paper in 1896, Hawke and Jackson in Yorkshire used the same dressing-room as the professionals, except when Gloucestershire had played recently at Bramall Lane and issued a request for the amateurs to have a room to themselves. Down at the Oval, however, there does not even seem to have been a whiff of reform in the air about these and similar arrangements differentiating the two species. The received wisdom has always been that most people at the time accepted such arrangements as part of the 'natural' order of things, but it is worth quoting part of a letter that appeared in the *St James's Gazette* in 1890 from Major-General G. F. I. Graham:

> It has always struck me as very invidious that any difference should be made between amateur and professional cricketers when making their entrance to the cricket-field. At present the invariable rule is that the professionals make their appearance out of a hole-in-the-corner sort of passage, while the amateurs come proudly down the centre of the pavilion.

On tour, of course, the distinctions were equally marked, with the amateurs staying in better-class hotels or, quite often, being put up by clubs or garrisons. One moment in Abel's Surrey career that may have made him feel a tinge of bitterness occurred in 1886, when the Prince of Wales turned up to watch the last hour of the first day's play against the Australians and was subsequently introduced to the tourists, plus Messers J. Shuter, W. W. Read, and W. E. Roller. But really the unblinking fixture list of 1890 said it all, announcing that Cambridge University were to be pitted against Gentlemen of England, with Pougher: there were few prizes for guessing who would do most of the bowling.

What made a Gentleman? When in the autumn of 1888 Major Warton was completing the arrangements for his tour to the Cape, he wrote to his prospective captain, C. Aubrey Smith:

> I hope sincerely that we may be able to arrange a *modus vivendi*, but at the same time do not see my way to offering you similar terms to Mr Bowden. My arrangement with him is practically a private matter. I did not anticipate at the outset that any of the amateurs would require more than travelling

and hotel expenses – and I may say that with the exception of Bowden this is the case.

Eventually a *modus vivendi* was reached: but the Major had shown himself to be a shade naïve and should have realized that there were amateurs and amateurs, that in other words not everyone who for reasons of social background wished to play under that unpaid guise could in fact afford to do so. 'Commercial travellers' was apparently the Old Buffer's term for certain amateurs; while in 1898, when the Gentlemen met the Players at the Oval, *The Times* described it as a fixture which 'in these days when the line between amateurs and professionals is so fine, has lost much of its old interest'. In an article in the *Daily Express* in 1903, Fry discussed the controversial question of amateurs' expenses. He distinguished between 'the amateur who is a salaried treasurer or secretary', which undoubtedly existed and was a matter of opinion as to its legitimacy, and actual under-the-counter payments by the club ('surreptitious bank-notes found in boots'), which according to Fry were a journalistic fancy. The usual practice, he asserted, was that county clubs 'one and all pay their amateurs out-of-pocket expenses', i.e. hotel bills and railway tickets. And 'no amateur, however clever he may be at accounts, has yet succeeded in going through a cricket season without being considerably out of pocket at the finish'.

The glaring exception to Fry's rule was, of course, W. G. Grace. The financial facts of his career have been well documented: the £20 minimum match fee to play for Gloucestershire, the testimonials of £1,400 and over £9,000, and the trip to Australia in 1891–92 that cost Lord Sheffield £3,000 in addition to expenses for Grace, his wife, and two children, plus the cost of a locum for his practice. When he failed to appear for the South of England versus the Australians at Hastings in 1886, the local paper said that 'it was understood that Mr W. G. Grace demanded too high a figure for his services'. He was, inescapably, the star attraction on all grounds, and demanded to be rewarded accordingly – a fact that the Surrey committee recognized when in 1891 it decided that 'with the exception of Mr W. G. Grace no money be paid for expenses directly or indirectly to anyone representing Gentlemen versus Players either this year or hereafter'. In the mid-1890s, though, criticism began to mount about the blatant scale of the Doctor's shamateurism, causing a certain rethink of policy on the part of the Surrey committee. By a vote of five to four it decided in 1895 to give 50 guineas, not 100, to his second testimonial; and two years later the decision of 1891 making an exception of Grace in the matter of expenses was rescinded.

But if by the end of the century the great man's performances were at last waning and he could no longer make his own terms in quite the same way, the Surrey committee soon found that if it treated all the country's amateurs as well-to-do men of leisure, there would be few Gentlemen of any calibre left to meet the Players at the Oval. Thus in 1898 Townsend and Sewell each received £4 as expenses for playing in the Oval match, while four years later bats were presented to Beldam, McGahey, and W. G. himself for their scores for the Gentlemen. It was in general an area of cricketing life about which there was little explicit discussion, but C. A. Stein, a stockbroker who was a prominent member of Surrey's committee, did offer a certain perspective on the question when he told *Cricket* in 1903:

> Many of Surrey's most promising players are City clerks or in business – men who by education and general training object strongly to play as professionals. I may say that, personally, I am a strong advocate for the system of paid amateurs. In the old days people used to laugh at me when I said that the time *must* come when amateurs would have to be compensated for their loss of time, but the necessity for so doing is, I think, much more generally recognized now. But Surrey has determined to have nothing whatever to do with paid amateurs, whether other counties encourage them or not.

This was seemingly unhypocritical stuff, but in fact Surrey's amateurs were by no means as unpaid as Stein would have had his readers believe.

The staple lubricant, as Fry said, was out-of-pocket expenses. As far as Surrey was concerned, this system began in 1884, when 'it was resolved that the experiment be tried of paying for the expenses of the amateurs in out-matches, Mr Read taking charge of the accounts'. The experiment seems to have continued more or less

unchanged until 1897, when it was decided that the amateurs were
to be allowed 'extra expenses' if incurred while playing home
matches for Surrey, though not exceeding £1 a day. Finally, in
1903, shortly before Stein was interviewed, a new scale was settled
on for amateurs' expenses: twenty-five shillings a day plus travelling
expenses for out-matches, while for home matches (Lord's, Leyton
and Crystal Palace as well as the Oval) travelling expenses only. As
for the murky world of additional forms of inducement over and
above expenses, things were rarely so unequivocal as the minute of
September 1884 concerning E. J. Diver, an amateur who taught at
Wimbledon College: 'It was resolved that an additional sum of £30
be given to Mr Diver for his services during the past season and that
he receive a sum of £2 a week during the winter as long as he
remains in the county.' But two years later Diver took the unusual
(and brave) step of switching to professional status, describing
himself to the committee as 'extremely fond of cricket but not
having private means to allow me to continue playing as an amateur'.
In fact, he had not proved quite a good enough cricketer to make it
worth the committee's while to go on treating him as, in effect, a
paid amateur; and a few years later he moved as a professional to
Warwickshire.

The usual way of retaining an amateur's loyalty, though, was
neither by cash payments nor weekly winter retainers, but instead
took the form of 'presents', usually as a reward for meritorious
performances. In 1884 'it was resolved that a present of the value of
£25 be given to Mr Horner in recognition of his efficient bowling
during the season'; three years later, after Surrey had won the
Championship, it was decided that Shuter should receive a silver
service not exceeding fifty guineas in value, Key and Roller a silver
salver not exceeding ten guineas; and in July 1901 Crawford received
presumably resellable bats for each of his three recent centuries.
These presents could be fairly trifling: in 1886 'it was decided that
the framed photograph of the eleven which beat the Australians
on 31 July be given to each of the three amateurs who played,
an unframed to each of the professionals'. Getting married also
occasioned the committee's generosity, with thirty guineas for
Shuter in 1882 going up by 1888 to £50 for Key. There was also the
sometimes delicate question of jobs for the gentlemen. 'It was
resolved that Mr Bowden's entrance fees to the Stock Exchange as

a clerk to Mr Stein be paid, the amount not to exceed £50,' a minute of 1884 stated in connection with the somewhat impecunious Dulwich old boy. And around the turn of the century the case of V. F. S. Crawford became a minor *cause célèbre* in the cricketing world. Crawford came from a genteel, less than affluent background, being the son of the chaplain of the London County Asylum, showed brilliant promise as a batsman, and at least once threatened to go to Leicestershire as assistant secretary (which he eventually did). Thus in 1898 it was 'resolved that assistance be give to Mr V. F. S. Crawford to be employed in a stockjobber's office', though exactly what assistance the minutes do not reveal. Something must eventually have leaked, to judge by the presidential remarks at Surrey's A. G. M. in 1901:

> Lord Alverstone [formerly Webster] said that the Surrey club had made no arrangement of any kind with regard to Mr Crawford. What had happened was that a few gentlemen – some on the committee, and some not – had taken steps to start Mr Crawford in his business career, but that was all. He himself had subscribed a very small amount, and he thought that if exception was taken to such friendly acts as this, there would be an end to sport in England.

Surrey's supreme shamateur, though, during most of Abel's career was undoubtedly the county's so-called assistant secretary. In his column in *Cricket*, Holmes wrote in 1894:

> One county pays an amateur a salary of £250 for playing cricket, though this sum is ostensibly given him for the discharge of official duties, which he no more fulfils than I do. Expenses are also allowed, and of the most liberal order, besides a free pass between his home and the county ground. Say what we will, he is simply the best-paid professional in his county, though he comes out of the central gate of the pavilion, and gets an occasional touch of the cap from the professionals.

Holmes was almost certainly referring to W. W. Read and more or less got his facts right. Until 1881 Read had only been able to play for Surrey during the school holidays, when he could get away from assisting in his father's school at Reigate, but his appointment that year as assistant secretary turned him into a regular player. His original salary was £120, increased in 1883 to £150. In addition he received, as Holmes said, not only his season ticket from Reigate to London, but also from 1886 a regular autumn *honorarium* of £100 for his performances during the season. Furthermore, he began at some point, in lieu of any further increase in his formal salary, to receive a match fee of four guineas. There were other odd bonuses too: in 1884 'some articles of the value of 20 guineas in recognition of his fine innings for England against Australia' at the Oval; the following year a wedding present of £250 plus a clock; and in 1894 a grant by Surrey of £25 to Reigate Priory CC for the improvement of their ground. Read's secretarial responsibilities supervising the expenses of his fellow-amateurs allowed him to get away for the occasional winter tour: in 1887–88, according to the *Athletic News*, he received £1,317 10s for going to Australia, of which £1,000 was for his services and the rest for expenses; and four years later he co-arranged a tour to the Cape which eventually resulted in a court case over its financing, revealing that Read had received £850 in addition to his expenses.

Surrey's most substantial single gesture to him came in 1895 when it resurrected the Surrey versus England fixture, gave it to him as his testimonial, and themselves put £200 into the fund. The match receipts totalled some £700 and Read eventually received just over four figures from his testimonial. There was, however, a revealing safety clause in Surrey's agreement to give him what was in effect a benefit, namely that 'it be an understanding in the arrangement that the assistant secretaryship of the club held by him come to an end on his ceasing to be a regular member of the Surrey eleven'; and the following year the club decided that Read's time was up. With his assistant secretaryship deemed to be ending in December 1896, the committee in November offered him a lump sum of £375 by the following March 'in lieu of all future payments for salary, season tickets, allowance of £100, and match money'. Read replied that £375 was an under-estimate of his average earnings in previous years, 'viz. £150 salary, £100 donation, £120 average match money, and £28 season ticket, making in all £398'. Eventually the club gave him a £400 pay-off, thus ending a potentially ungentlemanly squabble.

What about the professionals proper? 'Never mind, Fred, go

upstairs and get your money – it's only a game,' said Braund in immortal words to Tate in 1902. Most pros were indeed paid on a match basis, by the 1880s usually £5 for a county match (plus £1 for a win) and up to £10 for a representative contest, though several counties also gave their players a small summer wage as ground-bowlers. In addition there was of course talent money, for a batsman usually a sovereign for every 50 runs. A good pro would help another out if he could, as when Chatterton made 51 not out for the Players at the Oval in 1898: 'He had to thank Abel for reaching his 50, the Surrey professional making no effort to score during Fry's last over, when only three runs more were wanted.' In an article in the journal *Labour History* (1972), W. F. Mandle estimates that by the end of the century a first-class professional was getting roughly £275 for a five-month season. Out of this, however, he had to pay for his own equipment and, more seriously, the expenses entailed in out-matches. One columnist in the *Athletic News* in 1896 reckoned that after paying his expenses the average county professional did not make much more than £100 from a season, while another in the *Daily Express* in 1903 stated that a Lancashire professional going on tour to Canterbury and Leyton might expect to spend £5 on travel and hotels out of the £13 he earned (two match fees of £6 each and a win bonus). So even though an extra £1 was increasingly tacked on to the match fee in the case of out-matches, this hardly covered expenses. Writing in the *Athletic News*, also in 1903, 'A County Cricketer' bemoaned the hidden extras: 'The "tips" the professional gives are legion, from "boots" at the hotel to "boots" on the ground; then there are waiters, cabs, and porters, all to come in turn.' And in particular there was the problem the London pro faced getting to and from the mainline station: 'The common or garden bus will not take his cricket bag and Gladstone, and the underground seldom suits. Nine times out of ten it is the ever useful shoful he has to hire, and that is not the cheapest method.'

It would perhaps be reasonable to conclude that by the beginning of the century an established county professional might hope to clear circa £120–150 from a season, a player of international standard nearer £200. Such sums were appreciably more than the approximate £95 a year that an unskilled town or agricultural labourer earned and could even be a little above the annual earnings of most skilled artisans. The problem with being a professional cricketer was not so much that it paid poorly, at least in comparison with the jobs of other working-class men, but that there was little provision, apart from the rather ineffectual Cricketers' Fund Friendly Society, for when that very specialized money-earning ability came to an end. For some it was an unbearable prospect, one that not even Scotton could stonewall his way out of, killing himself at the age of thirty-seven after losing his place in the Nottinghamshire eleven. Any professional with nous would have been acutely conscious that while still playing he should try to earn as much as he possibly could.

At the Oval in Abel's time the only salaried professional was, as befitted his background as well as his abilities, the hard-headed Lohmann, who for a brief period in the 1890s was on £300 a year. However, there were during the summer the ground-bowlers' wages paid to the professionals: details in the Surrey minute books are somewhat patchy (as they also are about the match fees as such), but Abel's wage as an increasingly senior, and presumably increasingly nominal, ground-bowler seems to have increased in the course of the 1890s from £1 weekly to £2 weekly. A further symbol of the professionals not being wholly casual labour was the principle, especially important to fast bowlers, of their being paid for matches in which they stood down for physical rather than playing reasons. Thus when Abel in 1900 missed five consecutive matches because of his hand injury, 'it was decided that he should receive half-pay in two matches according to precedent'. There were also, of course, the occasional bonuses in addition to the regular payments by the executive: Abel in 1886 received £5 as well as an unframed photograph for his major part in defeating the Australians, rather more than most of his colleagues; while in 1890, after the Notts match, the committee voted each of the professionals £10. As for the talent money system operated by Surrey, there were intermittent moves towards giving the captain a free hand to reward his players as he thought fit, but generally the conventional scale appears to have remained the rule. It is said (but not documented) that when Abel made his record score in 1899, he received only £5 talent money, and subsequently remarked that in future he would not bother to go on once he had reached 250. The Oval crowd that day, though small, was rather more generous, mustering a collection of just over £33 in recognition of Abel's triple century.

This was one of six times in his career that a batting performance by him earned the spontaneous tribute of a collection – a figure that would almost certainly have been greater but for the fact that the committee had to give its sanction before a hat could go round the Oval. Big stands in 1886 and 1889 against the Australians and Notts, in which he was partnered by Maurice Read and Lockwood respectively, gained him a half-share in collections of £68 and £42. In 1897 his double century against Notts had his fellow-professionals going round the ground collecting a total of over £62 for him; while a few weeks later he and Brockwell shared a sum of £36, though quite apart from the Anglo-Indian's liverish response, there were, according to *The Times*, 'sundry rumours in the pavilion against this collecting business being rather overdone'. And finally, in 1899, a couple of months after the 357, he and Hayward received just under £73 for their partnership against Yorkshire, the monotony of the proceedings notwithstanding. Abel's trundling never inspired a collection, but in 1892 he did win a £25 prize from *Tit-Bits* for being top of the bowling averages one heady month.

All professional cricketers had, of course, the problem of what to do in the winter. Abel himself spoke on this theme in 1888, in a not altogether genuine-sounding interview printed in the *Star*:

> Professionals generally find something to do, but it occasionally happens that a good man is in low water before cricket commences in the spring. Lord Harris, I remember, once expressed the opinion that, after a cricketer had played with a county all the summer, they ought not to expect him to exhaust all his resources in the winter, but find him some employment on the ground or elsewhere. This matter is certain to meet with the attention it deserves before long.

The problem might have been particularly serious for Abel in the early to mid-1880s, when he earned appreciably less during the summer months than was later the case, but as it happened his snubbed benefactor in the hop warehouse turned the other cheek. As Abel told Bettesworth about the time he had gone up to the Oval, 'although Mr Wrigley professed to be greatly annoyed with me, he used to take me back in the winter, which was a generous thing to do'.

Abel's situation was further improved from 1887, when Surrey began her great run of success and the committee started giving an autumn bonus to the professionals for services rendered, with the exact amount per player determined in consultation with the captain. Abel usually did better than most of his colleagues, with the invariable exception of Lohmann, and over the years received an average of about £30 from this annual handout. In 1893, though, when Surrey fared disastrously, 'Mr Everett's proposition to grant a sum not exceeding £100 among the professional members of the county team was not carried.' The committee's decision – implying that the autumn bonus was a reward, not a right – was no doubt taken in the context of the fact that Surrey had recentlyintroduced a form of winter wages, probably as pioneered by Lord Hawke in Yorkshire. The precise date of the scheme's introduction is unclear, but a minute for November 1892 records it being successfully recommended 'that Abel, Wood, Watts, Henderson, and Smith be engaged on the ground during the winter in the interest of Surrey cricket. Abel, Wood, and Henderson to receive thirty shillings a week, Watts and Smith the same as last winter.' For the rest of his playing career Abel received a winter wage of thirty shillings. The wage was essentially a retainer, and it is unlikely that apart from some odd tasks he and the others had to do all that much to earn it, though it is noteworthy that in 1896 Street had ten shillings docked off his winter wage because he was not prepared to come to the Oval.

In the autumn of 1903 the committee held an inquiry into the question of winter employment. Excluding Abel himself, and the Australia-bound Hayward and Strudwick, it transpired that out of the fifteen professionals (including Hobbs) currently on winter wages, only three had a winter job: Rushby was a carpenter, Stedman a bricklayer, and Gooder a paperhanger. The findings clearly surprised the committee, for at the following spring's AGM, 'speaking on the subject of winter pay for the professionals, Lord Alverstone quite approved of the system, but he was very strongly of opinion that it was desirable for cricketers not to depend entirely on the game, but to have some occupation during the winter months.' But then, he had never been a bricklayer trying to get piece-work during the worse time of the year.

However, for leading professionals there was always the hope of a tour as a winter escape route. When Abel went to the Cape in 1888–89, he and the other professionals seem to have got the same terms as Bowden procured, namely £100 plus expenses, though of course Bowden would be staying at different hotels and travelling in better-lit carts. The terms may not have been all that glittering, but the tour in fact proved extremely profitable to Abel: there was an abundance of money slopping around South Africa at the time, first-class English cricketers were a great novelty, and he was easily the tourists' leading batsman. Apart from the ten guineas collected by the Grahamstown spectators, he also received, amongst other things, £20 and a diamond at Kimberley, £20 and a gold medal at Port Elizabeth, and fifteen gold-mine shares at Johannesburg. Also at Johannesburg, he and Frank Hearne received £45 from Cecil Rhodes, who had wagered against long odds that the two batsmen would knock off without loss the 137 required to beat the local team. 'I never saw such presents – so costly, rich, and rare,/Their sterling worth and beauty baffled me,' the Surrey Poet was moved to write after he had gone round to Abel's house on the team's return home.

As for Abel's two tours to Australia, details are not known of what he received, but it would not have been more than about a tenth of what W. G. commanded in 1891–92. Some guide is given in Barlow's autobiography, where he reveals that in three trips to Australia during the 1880s he was paid, in addition to all first-class expenses, £220 twice and £320 once. Abel's great financial moment on his tours came after he had carried his bat at Sydney in 1892, when 'Lord Sheffield was so pleased that he made out a cheque for £50 [presumably not post-dated to after the match] and handed it to the diminutive Surrey man'. He could have gone a third time to Australia, being offered £300 plus expenses by Stoddart in 1894, but held out for £500, which he did not get. This show of intransigence is perhaps explained by the fact that he was no longer so dependent for off-season income on the Borough warehouse and/or winter wages. He was instead turning into a man of business.

'In 1894 I laid down an extensive bat-making plant adjoining my shop against the Oval,' Abel recorded in his memoirs. According to Pridham, he obtained his willow from the Norfolk estate of the sometime Speaker of the House of Commons, Lowther, who used to like to stop at the Oval for some batting practice on his way to Westminster. Abel's partner in the early years of his business, when it was based at 310 Kennington Road, was J. Lane, who for the previous twenty-five years had been with E. J. Page & Co. *Cricket* in 1897 reviewed the initial progress of Abel's enterprise:

He has not let the grass grow under his feet. His bat, named 'The Guv'nor', has been a success, while the patent ball has deservedly made its way. It is Abel's intention to cater for footballers during the winter, and a special ball may be looked for.

The patent cricket ball was of the softer variety, which, as Abel himself told Bettesworth that same year, was especially designed for Board School children. He had one fairly steady market for his equipment: at a Surrey committee meeting in 1896, 'a letter was read from Abel sending samples of cricket balls of his manufacture, and it was decided to buy three sent'. The following year he sold the club a dozen balls, while in 1898 Abel & Lane beat off the estimates of various other firms, including Baldwin & Marshall, and supplied five nets. Then in January 1902, at the same committee meeting that considered Apted's defence of his liquid mixture, 'a letter was read from Robert Abel stating that he had dissolved partnership with Mr Lane, that he had taken on the business himself, and asking permission to have a small case placed in the players' room to show a few bats, balls, and pads and gloves.' Perhaps surprisingly, 'the request was granted, the Secretary to see to the details'. Abel & Son, as the firm became, apparently flourished in 1902, again defeating several rival estimates for selling nets to the Surrey club and in May even taking over the cricket business run by Baldwin, who was becoming coach at Uppingham School.

Abel had certainly followed a time-honoured course by starting a sports shop business: amongst a host of professional cricketers, Daft, Shaw, Shrewsbury, Gunn, Watson, Briggs and Sugg all did the same. But according to Craig in *Cricket Comicalities*, published in 1899, there was one person who was not so convinced about the wisdom of his action:

Discussing Bobby Abel's ill success at the early part of this season, my landlady startled me by saying she knew he would 'go off'. 'Why?' I inquired. 'Well,' she replied, 'you see he *makes* cricket bats and balls now and sees too much of 'em.

It's only natural that he can't do his self justice. I'm sure I
never eats a good dinner when I cooks it meself.'

One way and another the mid-1890s represented a key phase in
Abel's life: on the field he unexpectedly entered into his prime as a
batsman; off it he began his sports equipment business; and in 1895
he experienced the most arbitrary, but also momentous three days
in any professional's career – the benefit match, an occasion which
it had not yet become customary to insure against bad weather.
Mandle has provided various figures for the period, showing that
benefits in Yorkshire and Lancashire were usually significantly
higher than elsewhere: thus in 1893 Tunnicliffe's £1,750 compared
favourably to Shrewsbury's £600, in 1901 Brown's £2,282 likewise
to Lilley's £850. Before 1895 the record of Surrey's beneficiaries
was fairly indifferent: for instance, Richard Humphrey in 1885
made only £81, Beaumont in 1892 only £100, while in 1883 and 1894
Pooley and Wood respectively each cleared a moderate £450. The
only real exception was Maurice Read, who in 1893 was given half
the gate of the England versus Australia match and altogether
made about £1,200. Poor Harry Wood a year later must have been
especially envious, with his 'chosen' North versus South match at
the Oval being vitiated by the committee's insistence on charging
one shilling for admission, as was usual there for representative
matches, despite Wood requesting a sixpenny charge; and, as a
result, less than 10,000 paid at the gate over the three days to watch
a rather lacklustre contest. In Abel's case, the committee resolved
in October 1894 that he 'be allowed any match but the Bank
Holiday match', the invariable exception. A few weeks later he sent
them the following letter (original spelling):

As you cannot see your way clear to give me the August Bank
Holliday match I have decided with your kind permission to
have the Surrey *v* Yorkshire match for my benifit. There is
one favour gentlemen I do hope you will be able to grant me &
that is to brake your rule & give me the stand money. In asking
this I can only remind you of my past services. Also the two
benifit matches in one season [a reference to the Surrey versus
England match arranged for W. W. Read's testimonial] & the
fact that I have a wife & six children to provide for, my

oldest son being under thirteen years of age. By granting my request before the season commences I need hardly say you would take a deel of anxiety off my mind & secure me to some extent against wet weather.

The letter failed to tug the heart-strings: 'It was resolved that Abel have the match Surrey *v* Yorkshire for his benefit, but that his application for stand money could not be granted.' And there Abel's benefit more or less rested until the match itself, though at the same committee meeting in June 1895 at which it was decided to give £200 to W. W. Read's testimonial and debated as to whether W. G.'s should receive 100 guineas or 50, it was also mooted that £50 should be the size of the grant to be subscribed to Abel's fund.

The Yorkshire match started on 12 August, a Monday, and was literally the day of the silver lining, 'the Oval being about the only place that escaped from the downpours that prevailed in the immediate neighbourhood'. The match itself was important, the beneficiary popular, and over 18,000 attended, of whom 15,301 paid their sixpence at the gate. The Tuesday proved a wash-out: heavy rain in the morning was too much for the brightness of the afternoon to overcome and, in the words of the *Athletic News*, Abel was 'quite broken-hearted when there was no prospect of play'. However, his spirits perhaps recovered the next day, when play was resumed and 9,865 people paid at the gate. Moreover, to quote one of the many sympathetic match reports detailing his relative misfortune: 'The fact of adverse weather spurred Abel's friends up very considerably, and some of them trotted round with the boxes on Wednesday, when upwards of £60 was collected. The "Bard" was especially energetic, and "addressed meetings" nearly all day long.' In the end he probably earned about £730 from his benefit: comprising £486 from the gate after expenses had been deducted, £134 subscribed by members, £60 collected from the crowd, and £50 from the committee. It was not exactly a golden pay-out, but Wood for one would not have sneezed at it. Other Surrey beneficiaries later in the decade tended to fare better, with Lohmann, Henderson, and Richardson all going into four figures. Abel's sum would have been £131 17*s* 6*d* more if he had been allowed the stand money: a final request to the committee in November 1895 asking them to make an exception was turned down, as he must have known it would be. But as Abel also knew, it was not so much the lack of stand money that had half undone him as the capriciousness of the British climate and, it must be added, the benefit system itself.

The following year Abel was again in correspondence with the Surrey executive – and not just about samples of cricket balls. He was one of the five signatories (with Lohmann, Gunn, Hayward, and Richardson) of the letter dated Monday 3 August, that the committee considered three days later:

> Sir, we the following players having been asked to represent England *v* Australia August 10 and two following days do hereby take the liberty to ask for increased terms, viz. twenty pounds. The importance of such fixture entitles us to make this demand. Trusting this will meet with your approval . . .

The request did not, however, meet with the approval of the committee, who set about inviting other players to take the place of the troublesome five for the Third (and decisive) Test that was to begin at the Oval the following Monday. The story of the 1896 'strike' and the general background to it is fairly well-known. The five professionals wanted double the usual match fee for playing for England and probably had three main motives or grievances in mind as they pressed their claim: a deepening sense of vexation over the double standards of shamateurism; a feeling that the greatly increased size of cricket crowds over the previous decade or so ought to be reflected at least somewhat in the size of the match fees; and envy of the Australian players, who usually made about twice as much from coming to England as English players did from going down under. There had been withdrawals of labour before – in 1881 the famous Notts strike over general terms and in 1888 a threatened one by the Players, including Abel, unless they each received £20 for playing in a match against the Australians at the Oval – but this was by far the most dramatic, coming when it did.

In the end, Abel, Hayward and Richardson climbed down on the Saturday, placed themselves unreservedly 'in the hands' of the Surrey committee, and on the Monday morning, after a lengthy meeting chaired by the Surrey president, were reinstated into the England eleven. The meeting was so protracted not only because of the problem of the three theoretically repentant professionals, but also because two of the amateurs due to play, Grace as captain and Stoddart, were much put out by press and word-of-mouth rumours flying about over the weekend about their immoral earnings from

LONDON, THURSDAY, 13 AUGUST, 1896.

ASKING FOR MORE.
(With apologies to "Oliver Twist.")

Little "Oliver" Abel asks Mr. "Bumble" Surrey for more, and Dr. Grace is shocked.

cricket. Stoddart in fact withdrew from the team on the ostensible grounds of illness, while Grace played only after a statement had been issued by the Surrey club asserting that for representative matches at the Oval the only payment he had received was £10 designed to cover his travelling and hotel expenses. It must have been a tightly knit team that took the field for England.

The newspaper that dug deepest into the whole affair was the recently founded *Daily Mail*. On the Saturday before the match it included an interview with one of the striking Surrey players, who declined to be named but was probably Lohmann, generally recognised as the 'ring-leader'. His position was clear:

> We want £20 apiece and expenses. The Australians will probably take away £1,700 or £1,800, and the Surrey club will probably benefit to the same extent or more. We professional cricketers in England do not get anything like adequate payment for our services. The enormous crowds which now follow the game benefit the clubs and, in fact, everybody but those who have done at least their fair share towards bringing the game towards its present state – the professional players.

When questioned about the timing of the players' action, the interviewee described it as 'the most natural time . . . the time when most is going to be made out of us without anything like an adequate return'. And he went on to assert that 'the amateurs who are playing will be paid more than us professionals', i.e. 'the amateurs' expenses will exceed the payments or salaries of the professionals, and not for the first time by a long way'. With this scoop under his belt, the *Daily Mail* journalist tried for another:

> The news that a remodelled eleven had been chosen, omitting the four Surrey men and Gunn, came as a bolt from the blue upon one of the players at least, Robert Abel, the popular 'Little Guv'nor' of the Oval enthusiasts. He was seen at his residence, near the Oval, and he was at first most reluctant to utter a word. But when our representative told him the news [announced by Alcock on the Friday] that a new eleven had been chosen, he relinquished his policy of silence in sheer astonishment. Asked whether the dissatisfaction was of long duration, he replied that it was. 'So you seized this opportunity,' suggested our reporter, 'and calculated to get the club at your mercy, and to get higher wages for the future?' – 'No, that would not be a fair way of putting it. We had no desire to get the club at our mercy. It was only in respect of this match that we applied for better remuneration.' – 'But why for this

match?' – 'Well, I need hardly say it is a match of unusual importance. It is a matter of great anxiety to us when we know we are playing for England in a critical encounter, and our best and hardest play is required of us. That's why the application was made in this particular match.'

On the Saturday afternoon, at the Oval Hotel, the paper conducted a still more explicit interview with Harry Wood, which it published on the Monday. 'If I had taken to cricket as a "gentleman" I should have made sufficient out of my "expenses" to enable me to retire,' he asserted, after stating that from twenty years as a county professional he had saved nothing. Summer income was bitten deep into by the expenses involved in out-matches, while 'in the winter I've had to work here at the Oval at "turfing" for a wage of 26 shillings a week' and 'other professionals have had to stumble along through the winter months as well as they could'. Wood was particularly bitter about the lack of a pension fund for retired Surrey players, but it was to the shamateurs that he returned obsessively: 'We know that these gentlemen take their £20 and £30 and sometimes £50 a match, whilst we are kept down to our £5 and £6 – and don't you forget to deduct our expenses from that.' And he finished by talking about his benefit of two years earlier:

> The Surrey committee treated me very shabbily in that matter. They insisted on my taking a duffing North and South match, and I only got £350 [i.e. from the match itself], whereas with fair treatment I ought to have netted £1,000. I was shoved aside, I believe, to make way for Mr Shuter's testimonial.

Wood, not surprisingly, found himself being reprimanded a few days later by the Surrey committee, but by then the cat, as far as the cricket world at large was concerned, was well and truly out of the bag.

The orthodox view (as expressed in print) about the professionals' threatened strike was that though they had the intrinsic merits of the case on their side, the actual timing had been inappropriate. In the words of *The Times* on the Monday morning:

> Whatever the outcome of the dispute that has occurred, and however beneficial to the professionals in the end, the 'strike'

has been a great grief to the best lovers of the game. Loyalty to the Surrey club and patriotism for English cricket should have been a sufficient incentive to the players to have practised self-denial for a while longer'.

Or, as the *Daily Graphic* put it rather more sternly:

It was in every way a regrettable demonstration. If the players had held out, the last and most important of the Test matches with Australia would have been deprived of its representative character – to the disappointment of the public both in England and Australia. By the side of this consideration the question whether the players, who are in some sense the servants of the public, have or have not a grievance sinks to very small dimensions.

The four Surrey players (including Lohmann, who had withdrawn his demand too late to be reinstated in the team) sought to answer these and similar criticisms in a statement issued on the 11th. In the context of being 'blamed for waiting until the eve of the Test match before approaching the Surrey committee on the question of remuneration', the signatories pointed out that their original letter had not been considered until the 6th, three days after it had been received by Alcock, and that news of it had not been made public until the 7th. And they went on:

We express the hope that in future professionals will receive a higher wage in these important representative matches. We applied at Lord's *after* the first Test match, and were refused. At Manchester we asked for our expenses, which up to the present we have not received.

But if criticized in the editorial columns of the press, Abel and Co. had their supporters elsewhere. On the first day of the match, as the crowd waited for the rain to clear, the *Star* took the popular pulse: 'The talk round the ropes amongst the spectators is all about the great strike and its probable consequences. The voice of the people in this instance is unmistakably in favour of the professionals.' Though Craig in answer to questions from the ring maintained an attitude of studied neutrality, this general sympathy was again manifested the next day, as England batted twice. In the somewhat reluctant words of *The Times*: 'There was some curiosity as to how the spectators would receive Hayward, Richardson, and Abel, and it must be said that all three men were cheered as heartily as ever they were on the Oval.' Moreover, the stand that the professionals had taken did quite quickly have the desired effect. The Alverstone/Alcock 1902 volume on Surrey states that after the actual 1896 match each professional received £20 from the committee, though there is no mention of this in the minutes; while certainly from 1899 the standard rate for playing in a home Test became £20. 'Nice customs curtsey to great kings' was the aphorism cited by *Wisden* in 1897 to justify W. G.'s anomalous financial position, but eventually, though long after Abel's day, it would be the professionals who started to wear the crown.

Lord Harris once remarked that 'a professional cricketer rarely makes old bones'. It was an assertion that probably would have been challenged by Le Balafré, author of a sanguine article in *Cricket* in 1890 about the recent progress of the game:

> How about the many coloured shirts and pants of the cricketing professional twenty years ago? What an improvement may be seen, in the turn-out of the 'pro' of the present day. Take the Surrey team, as an instance, as they leave the pavilion. Are they not a picture, both for condition and style? M. Read lithe and active as a panther. 'Bobby' 'all there', and got up for the occasion. The immortal George, with nothing about him to stamp him as a 'pro', and yet in a condition that will carry him with ease through his three days' work.

Le Balafré's words are to an extent confirmed by some longevity statistics. If, for instance, one takes the forty-seven professionals who represented the Players at Lord's in the thirteen matches there between 1886 and 1902 in which Abel participated, their average life-span works out at a fairly respectable sixty-four years. By interesting comparison, the average life-span for the fifty-eight amateurs who represented the Gentlemen in the same matches was only three years longer. Few amateurs' families, though, would have found themselves in the same position as the wife and five children of George Davidson, who died of influenza in 1899 after twelve years with Derbyshire as an invaluable all-rounder, leaving nothing except £45 of the £200 he had received from his benefit.

It is impossible to make any precise comparisons between the respective wealth of the amateurs and professionals of Abel's time, but one *very* rough guide lies in the amount they left on death, as shown in the Somerset House records. Again taking as a working sample those cricketers who played in the Gentleman versus Players matches at Lord's featuring Abel, the following (necessarily incomplete) figures emerge: that 48 amateurs left between them a total of £1,574,870, averaging £32,809; and that 32 professionals mustered only £234,074 averaging £7,314. One must stress, though, the rough-and-ready character of the evidence, especially for those who died afer the First World War, when death duties began to bite and people started to transfer their wealth while still alive. But for what it is worth, the richest amateur is T. L. Taylor of Yorkshire (£241,639), followed by Hylton Philipson (£228,193) and F. H. E. Cunliffe (£149,209). Of those who died before 1918, W. G. left a surprisingly small £7,278 (though one must multiply by about twenty times to get the modern equivalent), Stoddart £1,060, and R. E. Foster £6,318. Among the professionals, the well-known bat-maker William Gunn led the way on £57,392, followed by Rhodes (£50,148) and W. G. Quaife (£18,500). Scotton left £242, Shrewsbury £7,649, Barlow £1,574, Ulyett £1,064, Ward £10,041, Richardson £629, Mold £549, and Hirst £5,844. The figures do not include Albert Trott, who, bankrupt, killed himself on the eve of the 1914 war, leaving his clothes to his landlady. Such a fate was a familiar enough one among the professionals of that era to explain why a matter of £10 could occasion the bitterness that it apparently did in 1896.

Abel in his final years as a first-class cricketer sensibly continued to diversify his activities, several times going to Leyton in April to give some pre-season coaching to the younger Essex players. McGahey, interviewed by *Cricket* in 1896, gave a certain insight into his methods:

> I never had any coaching until this year, when Mr Green sent Abel and Maurice Read to coach us at Leyton. It seemed very funny at first to be told that you mustn't do this and you mustn't do that, but it was, nevertheless, obvious that the advice was good and sound.

He probably cut his teeth as a coach on his children. 'One wondered whether, as in the first match against the Australians at the Oval, Bobby had got his son to give him an hour's bowling at home in the back garden,' speculated the *Star* in 1896 as he moved towards his century for Surrey. 'Father', incidentally, was the nickname given to Abel by W. G., who at the Oval one day had heard one of Abel's sons asking, 'Is father here?' In fact, two of Abel's sons subsequently played first-class cricket – William for Surrey, Tommy for Surrey and Glamorgan – but neither ever quite made the grade and both died in their forties.

What must have loomed increasingly large in family discussion, however, was the state of Abel's health, especially his eyes. 'Allow me to thank you all very kindly for your great kindness to me through my illness last winter & paying all my expenses during my stay at Ventnor and I am sorry I have not shewn a better result,' he wrote to the committee in July 1903. And the following year, with Abel's career palpably drawing to a speedy close, the committee decided to give him a testimonial, with a view to compensating him for his rather disappointing benefit match. The centre-piece of the testimonial took place on the first afternoon of the Bank Holiday match, when the other Surrey professionals went round the ground with collection boxes. Abel unfortunately had already been dismissed for 1, but the collection still realized a few shillings under £100. Another ground collection on the second day produced a further £57. In the end his testimonial fund amounted to £464, including £50 from the committee and the receipts of £157 from a match held at the Oval between jockeys and amateur athletes. Following the recent practice initiated in Yorkshire by Lord Hawke, almost half the fund was invested by the committee on Abel's behalf, in Mexican 4 per cent Scrip. Stein must have reckoned it was a reasonably gilt-edged proposition.

Odd details survive about Abel's years of retirement. Apart from the occasional game for the Club and Ground up to 1907, he seems to have played little serious cricket. He did not (c.f. Ross in *The Surrey Story*) play for Surrey against Oxford University at Reigate in 1909: the Abel was one of his sons. His eyesight was continuing to deteriorate, a fact that caused his appointment in 1907 as coach to Surrey's young players to end after one year and similarly interfered with the coaching he also undertook at Dulwich College. During the exigencies of the war, he was employed at £2 a week to bowl to and coach Surrey's schoolboy members; but in 1921 the match committee, no doubt regretfully, 'recommended that an application from R. Abel for an engagement as coach to boys at the Oval be not granted'.

On the literary front he collaborated with the sporting journalist-cum-publisher H. V. Dorey to produce the collection of Craig's rhymes as well as his own reminiscences, one of the first of the 'told to' cricket autobiographies. He also took the opportunity, in 1909, of persuading the somewhat reluctant Surrey committee to give him the balance of his testimonial money. If that money was still locked up in Mexican shares, it was fortunate that he did so, for the revolution there soon afterwards would have sent them tumbling. The reason given to the committee was that he wanted 'to extend his business'; but by the early 1920s at the latest the affairs of Abel & Son seem to have gone into irreversible decline. It was not the mellowest of old ages: Sarah Abel died in 1923, aged sixty-two, while Abel himself by this time was close to blindness. 'The secretary reported that R. Abel was again in difficulties,' the minutes of the finance committee record for 1926; and in January 1927 'it was decided that the Surrey club make no claim against R. Abel for sums advanced to him in July 1925 and September 1926 amounting to £88 2*s* 8*d*'. Fortunately there was a happy outcome. Once again the *Daily Mail* was best placed to tell the story, which it did in April 1927:

The affairs of 'Bobby' Abel, the veteran England and Surrey cricketer, who found himself in straitened circumstances, have now been settled. His business as an athletic outfitter has been sold to Mr Charles Riggs of Bishopsgate, who has arranged to retain Mr Abel in an advisory capacity, and the funds subscribed for him have been expended. The committee who conducted the settlement state that the committee of the Surrey club long ago decided against doing anything to save Abel's business, but promised him that as soon as he could dispose of his business they would provide for him. The *Daily Mail* Fund (amounting to £1,010 0*s* 9*d*) has enabled the committee to settle with the creditors of R. Abel & Son, to repay the mortgages on Mr Abel's house, and to provide an annuity of approximately 17*s* 6*d* per week. To this the Surrey committee will add a further annuity from funds in their possession and a weekly pension, all of which combined will ensure for Mr Abel comfort for the remainder of his life.

He must have been warmed by the response to the fund that the paper had set up for him: a thousand pounds for a player who had retired over twenty years earlier was a remarkable token of his abiding place in the cricketing public's affections.

If such are the bare facts of Abel's old age, a few anecdotes give some flavour. One was told by Leveson-Gower in his memoirs:

An amusing side-issue occurred during the police-hunt which ensued after Crippen and Miss le Neve vanished. I was talking one day to Bobby Abel and I remarked: 'I do not wish to be personal, but you know there is a great hunt for Crippen, and from the photographs which have appeared in the newspapers, people might say that there is a resemblance between you and him. Under the circumstances, perhaps it would be as well to keep to the house for a few days.' He replied with his usual modesty: 'Thank you kindly, sir; I will!' And I believe he did. Abel was at that time wearing spectacles, and though I spoke rather in joke, it was true that there was a considerable likeness, and in the excitement caused by the affair, it was not impossible that some mistake might have been made.

Another oft-told story concerned the fast-bowling skeleton in Abel's cupboard:

After retiring from active participation in the game, Abel was watching a match at the Oval when a professional batsman lost his wicket through palpably withdrawing from the line of the ball. 'You didn't like that one, did you?' chaffed Bobby, as the disconsolate player reached the pavilion. This was too much for the batsman, who was goaded to retort: 'You didn't run away in your time, did you, Bobby?' 'Well,' said the imperturbable little man, 'perhaps I did. But I'll tell you the difference between you and me. I used to leave my bat behind, you take yours with you!'

This version was told by Lieutenant-Colonel French, but Major Pridham had a variant that specifically named Abel's reputed *bête noir*. It told of Abel in the Oval pavilion, 'still wearing his faded

Surrey cap', watching the failures of the English batsmen in 1921 against the Australian fast bowlers and 'shaking his head sadly', which prompted one of the batsmen to accuse him: 'Oh yes, Bobby, *you* never ran away from fast bowling, did you? There was once a man called Kortright.' Whereupon he replied with his telling comparison of what he and his latter-day counterpart did with their respective bats. Colonel Trevor in one of his books tells a similar version, but perhaps more plausibly dates it to only a few years after Abel had retired.

The final anecdote is again the subject of two versions, though it is possible that the episode took place twice. One was told by Robertson-Glasgow in a 1945 piece called 'Oval Snapshots':

> I remember sitting by Sammy Woods at the Oval not long after the Kaiser's war; on his other side sat Bobby Abel, so small, and nearly blind; and Sammy, with his natural kindness, was recalling Bobby's great innings. 'Ah, Mr Woods,' said Bobby, 'the times you nearly knocked my head off.' 'And,' replied Mr Woods, 'the times, Bobby, you flicked me off your ear-hole to the square-leg boundary.'

Woods himself provides the variant, describing in his autobiography a visit to Abel 'at his shop near the Oval' after they had both retired:

> 'Hullo, Bobby, how are you?' 'Lor, it's Mister Sam; and the times you have nearly knocked my head off is wonderful, isn't it?' I said: 'Yes, my dear, and the times you have made my arm ache is wonderful, too!'

The Guv'nor abdicated on 10 December 1936, at the age of seventy-nine. He had been in poor health for some time and lay unconscious at his home in Handforth Road for the final twenty-four hours. He left £864 9*s* 7*d*. His funeral was held a week later at St Mark's Church, Kennington, and amongst those who attended was William Bradley. There was only one place for him to be buried: at Nunhead he joined not only Jupp and Craig, but also his wife and three children who had predeceased him. By an ironic fate for such an urbanite, the part of the cemetery where Abel lies is now being turned into a nature reserve for children and will soon be completely overgrown.

ABEL'S CAREER FIGURES

(First-Class Matches Only)

BATTING

	Matches	Innings	Times Not Out	Runs	Highest Innings	Average
1881	3	5	0	17	12	3.40
1882	16	27	3	176	31	7.33
1883	17	30	4	530	63	20.38
1884	16	29	2	486	68	18.00
1885	23	36	1	725	92	20.71
1886	27	47	5	1221	144	29.71
1887	22	34	0	638	92	18.76
1887–88	8	14	1	320	95	24.61
1888	29	44	2	1323	160	31.50
1888–89	2	3	1	189	120	94.50
1889	25	43	5	1095	138	28.81
1890	20	31	1	914	151*	30.46
1891	24	35	1	1139	197	33.50
1891–92	8	12	2	388	132*	38.80
1892	26	41	1	1108	117	27.70
1893	16	30	3	488	54*	18.07
1894	31	47	5	1447	168*	34.45
1895	32	50	4	2057	217	44.71
1896	35	55	3	2218	231	42.65
1897	32	50	3	2099	250	44.65
1898	30	45	3	2053	219	48.88
1899	35	53	3	2685	357*	53.70
1900	31	49	3	2592	221	56.34
1901	38	68	8	3309	247	55.15
1902	41	64	8	2299	179	41.05
1903	10	18	0	314	61	17.44
1904	20	34	1	839	87	25.42
Total:	617	994	73	32669	357*	35.47

BOWLING

	Overs	Balls	Maidens	Runs	Wickets	Average
1881	40	160	15	50	2	25.00
1882	189.1	757	79	298	12	24.83
1883	163	652	70	243	9	27.00
1884	187	748	73	301	16	18.81
1885	294.2	1178	107	488	21	23.23
1886	239	956	105	370	16	23.12
1887	340.3	1363	155	516	25	20.64
1887–88	29	116	9	46	1	46.00
1888	155	620	80	222	4	55.50
1888–89	–	–	–	–	–	–
1889	38	190	9	89	1	89.00
1890	58	290	18	119	4	29.75
1891	67	335	19	145	8	18.12
1891–92	–	–	–	–	–	–
1892	170.3	853	40	429	31	13.83
1893	115	575	31	276	12	23.00
1894	130.4	654	35	332	15	22.13
1895	84.1	421	24	216	4	54.00
1896	290	1450	99	606	31	19.54
1897	111	555	38	264	8	33.00
1898	55.2	277	19	132	4	33.00
1899	155.3	778	48	384	14	27.42
1900	58.4	352	9	203	6	33.83
1901	95.4	574	24	302	8	37.75
1902	16	96	1	62	2	31.00
1903	–	–	–	–	–	–
1904	7.1	43	0	49	0	–
Total:	c.3090.3	13993	1107	6142	254	24.18

ABEL IN VERSE

THREE POEMS BY ALBERT CRAIG:

1 *Abel, Our Surrey Champion, Safe Home Again From Africa,*
  20 April 1889

> I've seen our genial favourite, our champion with the bat –
> Since Abel's safe arrived from the Cape;
> He's quite prepared for action, I'm glad to tell you that,
> He's never long in getting into shape.
> I hasten'd to Bermondsey last Tuesday afternoon,
> He told me that where'er he chanc'd to roam,
> The end of his engagements never came too soon,
> He loved to reach his dear old English home.
>
> Brave, upright, little batsman – courageous, cautious, true,
> Such men may 'Good Old Surrey' never lack;
> In walk, or talk, or action, we're not ashamed of you –
> 'God bless you, Bob!' we're glad to see you back.
> I never saw such presents – so costly, rich, and rare,
> Their sterling worth and beauty baffled me;
> It proves to us, old favourite, you did your duty there.
>   Believe me, Bob,
>   Your faithful friend.

2 *Robert Abel. Surrey's Pride. Brighton, 13 July 1891*

>   Watch his drives today;
>   Cuts for fours and threes;
>   And you'll witness a display
>   That cannot fail to please.
>   Bowlers bowl in vain,
>   Each man tries his hand,
>   Proudly at his post,
>   Still you see him stand.

Chorus: Well play'd Abel, good boy Bob,
You are fairly on the job;
Your position you retain,
Our little Champion is himself again.

Sturdy little 'brick',
    Active, staunch, and prim;
Gallantly you stick,
    Never out of trim.
Plaudits, long, and loud,
    Echo round the ring;
Every cricket crowd,
    Abel's praises sing.

3 *Abel, Everybody's Favourite. Secured 136 runs, not out, in*
the Surrey Match against Middlesex, 24 May 1894

Patiently our favourite plays,
Bowlers change, but still he stays,
Extra caution he displays,
    How they try to beat him.
Bowlers strive, but still they fail
To disturb a single bail.
Tell me, rare old Thoms and Gale,
    Is it wrong to greet him?

Chorus: Bravo, Abel, well-played Bob,
You are fairly on the job;
Your position you retain,
Our little Champion is himself again.

For three long and tedious hours
Abel shows great batting powers;
'Tis no bed of rosy bowers,
    'Twas a hard day's working.
Still the valiant little chap
Works away without mishap,
Never seems to care a rap,
    Duty never shirking.

Middlesex are no mean foe,
Byegone struggles clearly show
That proves Abel's pluck and go
    Has not yet diminished.
Bob, your place, you still retain,
May your judgement never wane,
Show your matchless form again,
    'E'er the season's finished.

ANONYMOUS VERSES PUBLISHED IN THE *ATHLETIC NEWS*, 1 JUNE 1903

Yuss, we've won a gime at lawst –
                Bobby's back,
And the nawsty toime is pawst –
                Bobby's back;
Surrey's browk the hevil spell,
Which the sime I'm pleased to tell;
Would yer koindly tech that bell?
                Bobby's back.

Ow, it wuz a norful strine –
                But Bobby's back;
And it guv me quoite a pine –
                Still Bobby's back.
In the lengwedge hof Mossoor,
We'd a 'movay quart de hoor',
But the trouble's gone, oi'm sure –
                Bobby's back.

Watch the bahndary for fours –
                Bobby's back;
Twig the pipers for big scores –
                Bobby's back!
Yorker, brike-back, leg-brike, lob,
Come aloike to Surrey's Bob;
'E's a doisy on the job –
                Bobby's back.

There ain't werry much o' 'im –
           But 'e's back;
And 'e's jest chock-full o' vim –
           Glad 'e's back.
When 'e's 'ittin' 'ard and free,
You can tike a tip from me
Them 'ere bowlers' glad to see
           Bobby's back.

So, old Surrey starts anew,
           'Cos 'e's back;
And she'll win a match or two
           Now 'e's back.
Wot? 'im a-gettin' old? O, rats!
One of Hengland's chisest bats.
'Ere, Eliza, chinge us 'ats!
           Bobby's back.

BIBLIOGRAPHY

BOOKS

Abel, Robert, *Cricket and How To Play It*, Dean, 1894.

Abel, Robert, *Life and Reminiscences of Robert Abel in the Cricket Field*, Cricket & Sports Publishers, 1910.

Alcock, C. W. (ed.), *Famous Cricketers and Cricket Grounds*, Hudson & Kearns, 1895.

Altham, H. S., *A History of Cricket*, Vol. 1, George Allen & Unwin, 1962.

Alverstone, Lord, and Alcock, C. W. (eds), *Surrey Cricket*, Longmans, 1902.

Arlott, John, *Vintage Summer: 1947*, Eyre and Spottiswoode, 1967.

Barlow, R. G., *Forty Seasons of First-Class Cricket*, Heywood, 1908.

Benson, E. F., and Miles, Eustace H., *The Cricket of Abel, Hirst, and Shrewsbury*, Hurst & Blackett, 1903.

Bettesworth, W. A., *Chats on the Cricket Field*, Merritt & Hatcher, 1910.

Brodribb, Gerald, *All Round the Wicket*, Sporting Handbooks, 1951.

Brookes, Christopher, *English Cricket*, Weidenfeld & Nicolson, 1978.

Brown, Lionel H., *Victor Trumper and the 1902 Australians*, Secker & Warburg, 1981.

Caffyn, William, *Seventy-One Not Out*, Blackwood, 1899.

Cardus, Neville, *Close of Play*, Collins, 1956.

Cardus, Neville, *Days in the Sun*, Rupert Hart-Davis, 1948.

Carew, Dudley, *England Over*, Martin Secker, 1927.

Collings, T. C. (ed.), *Cricket*, T. Fisher Unwin, 1900.

Craig, Albert, *Cricket and Football Rhymes, Sketches, Anecdotes, etc,* Cricket & Sports Publishers, 1910.

Craig, Albert, *Cricket Comicalities,* All England Athletic Publishing Co., 1899.

French, Lieut-Col. Gerald, *The Cornerstone of English Cricket,* Hutchinson, 1948.

Frith, David, *The Fast Men,* Van Nostrand Reinhold, 1975.

Fry, C. B., *Life Worth Living,* Eyre & Spottiswoode, 1939.

Fry, C. B. (ed.), *The Book of Cricket,* George Newnes, 1899.

Gale, Frederick, *The Life of the Hon Robert Grimston,* Longmans, 1885.

Giffen, George, *With Bat and Ball,* Ward Lock, 1898.

Gordon, Sir Home, *Background of Cricket,* Arthur Barker, 1939.

Grace, W. G., *Cricket,* Arrowsmith, 1891.

Grace, W. G., *W. G.: Cricketing Reminiscences and Personal Recollections,* James Bowden, 1899.

Hawke, Lord, *Recollections and Reminiscences,* Williams & Norgate, 1924.

Hodgson, R. L., (A Country Vicar), *Cricket Memories,* Methuen, 1930.

Hutchinson, Horace G. (ed.), *Cricket,* Country Life, 1903.

Iredale, Frank, *33 Years of Cricket,* Beatty, Richardson, 1920.

Jephson, D. L. A., *A Few Overs,* Heffer, 1913.

Jessop, Gilbert, *A Cricketer's Log,* Hodder & Stoughton, 1922.

Leveson-Gower, Sir Henry, *Off and On the Field,* Stanley Paul, 1953.

Lilley, A. A., *Twenty-Four Years of Cricket,* Mills & Boon, 1912.

Lyttelton, Hon. R. H., and others, *Giants of the Game,* Ward Lock, 1899.

Pridham, Major C. H. B., *The Charm of Cricket Past and Present,* Herbert Jenkins, 1949.

Ranjitsinhji, Prince, *The Jubilee Book of Cricket,* Blackwood, 1897.

Root, Fred, *A Cricket Pro's Lot,* Edward Arnold, 1937.

Ross, Gordon, *The Surrey Story,* Stanley Paul, 1957.

Sewell, E. H. D., *Who's Won the Toss?,* Stanley Paul, 1944.

Shaw, Alfred, *Alfred Shaw, Cricketer,* Cassell, 1902.

Standing, Percy Cross (ed.), *Cricket of Today and Yesterday,* 2 vols, Caxton Publishing Co (subscription illustrated edition), 1902.

Steel, A. G., and Lyttelton, Hon. R. H. (eds.), *Cricket,* Longmans, seventh edition, 1904.

Strudwick, Herbert, *Twenty-Five Years Behind the Stumps*, Hutchinson, 1926.

Travers, Ben, *94 Declared*, Elm Tree Books, 1981.

Trevor, Colonel Philip, *Cricket and Cricketers*, Chapman & Hall, 1921.

Warner, Sir Pelham, *Gentleman v Players 1806–1949*, Harrap, 1950.

Warner, Sir Pelham, *Long Innings*, Harrap, 1951.

Warner, Sir Pelham, *Lord's 1787–1945*, Harrap, 1946.

Woods, S. M. J., *My Reminiscences*, Chapman & Hall, 1925.

PERIODICALS AND NEWSPAPERS

Adelaide Observer
Argus (Melbourne)
Athletic News
Australasian
Birmingham Daily Post
Bradford Daily Telegraph
Brighton and Sussex Daily Post
Cape Times
Ceylon Observer
Cricket
Cricketer
Cricket Field
Daily Express
Daily Graphic
Daily Independent (Kimberley)
Daily Mail
Daily Telegraph (Sydney)
Derby Express
Derbyshire Times
Eastern Star (Johannesburg)
Empire
Evening Standard
Hastings and St Leonards Times
Journal (Grahamstown)

Leicester Daily Post
Leytonstone Express and Independent
Malta Times
Manchester Examiner and Times
Mercury (Hobart)
Morning Leader
Natal Mercury
Nottingham Daily Express
Port Elizabeth Telegraph
St James's Gazette
Scarborough Post
Sheffield Daily Telegraph
South London Journal
South London Press
Southwark Recorder
Sporting Life
Sportsman
Star
Taunton Echo
Taunton Mail
The Times
Western Daily Press
Westminster Gazette
Wisden Cricket Monthly

INDEX